alien
asian

simon tay

alien asian
a singaporean in america

°LANDM△RK°BOOKS°

This book is dedicated to Jin Huq,
even if it is not the novel she wanted.

Currency values are in US dollars
except where indicated.

© Simon Tay 1997
First published 1997

LANDMARK BOOKS PTE LTD
5001 Beach Road, #02–73/74
Singapore 199588

Landmark Books is an imprint of
Landmark Books Pte Ltd
ISBN 981–3065–08–7

Typecast by Superskill Graphics Pte Ltd
Printed by Loi Printing Pte Ltd

contents

preface

"It is often enough for a traveler (in Africa) . . . to say, more or less, 'This is me here. This is me getting off the old native bus and being led by strange boys, making improper proposals, to some squalid lodging. This is me having a drink in a bar with some local characters. This is me getting lost later that night.'

"This kind of traveler is not really a discoverer. He is more a man defining himself against a foreign background . . . Generally, though, this approach cannot work in the United States. The place is not and cannot be alien in the simple way an African country is alien. It is too well known, too photographed, too written about; and, being more organized and less informal, it is not so open to casual inspection."

V.S. Naipaul, *A Turn in the South*

I had an excuse for learning about America. Each fortnight for a year and a half, I wrote a column for the *Straits Times*, "Fax from America". Writing that column gave me a reason to focus on the country, to observe the society around me and to think about it, even if my main purpose there was to learn about international law, rather than about America. I learnt as much as I could before reducing everything to 1,000-word columns or less, so that each could be published in the newspapers back home, to an audience far away, across the Pacific. That, and the encouragement of people who enjoyed the articles I wrote, led to this book.

At first, the idea was to merely pull the newspaper columns together for a simpler, shorter book. But as I re-read them and re-thought my experiences, this became insufficient. The medium of journalism is not the same as a book. Nor is writing poetry or stories, which I was most used to. The task then became to re-open the incidents, to add people and detail, and to write about other happenings: all the things about America that the limitations of a newspaper column and its deadlines do not give you space or time for, and all the meaning within the strictures of real events and real people that fiction does not impose on you.

Every sentence that I had written abroad was re-examined and re-written, now in the context of being home in Singapore. In re-writing and re-thinking of America as I experienced it, I also had a recurring notion that gave this book its title, Alien Asian. The terms of the title may need some introduction but, I feel, they will be revealed in the book. Suffice it to say, as a preface, that "Alien" is the word that the USA officially uses to describe me and anyone who is not a citizen and does not live there. "Asian" is how the American mind lumps together and stereotypes people from the Indian sub-continent, East and Southeast Asia, and lands in-between, despite all their differences.

This book was written against the backdrop of an ongoing debate about East and West, Asian and American. Some argue that they are almost polar opposites in culture and politics. This book believes that there are bridges between the continents. It is based on the humanist belief that we can learn from each other, and can learn to appreciate each other.

In this book, all the incidents and people I have written about are drawn from life. Despite this, I do not claim that the book objectively describes America. There is no absolute objectivity. Whenever something is described or reported, there is the intermediary of the person who is making the observation. Therefore, Americans and others who know the country may disagree with this book. The people who are portrayed in this book may also disagree. They may remember the events with a different emphasis, from a different standpoint. They may not like my portrayals of them. If they are displeased with my descriptions of them, I apologise for that as unintended. At their request, I have used pseudonyms for some of them.

There are many people to thank for this book, of whom I can only name a few.

There are those who welcomed and befriended us in America: Karen and Linus Koh and their children; Ken Low and Danna Jennings; Chin Woon Ping, Duncan

Holaday and Rio; Don Snodgrass and his late wife, Ann; Benny and Junniper; Jacky and Yu Mian; and my classmates and professors at Harvard. Those who supported the scholarship that enabled my journey, Dennis Donohue, Domenick DiPasquale, Mike Anderson and their staff and successors at the US Information Service; and Prof. Chan Heng Chee, Prof. Tommy Koh, Dr Phillip Pillai, and Prof. Edwin Thumboo, my referees for the Fulbright scholarship. Back in Singapore, there are Richard Lim and others at Life! in the *Straits Times*, for their support of my column; my publisher, Goh Eck Kheng, for taking a risk with this type of travel book; my mother and family for keeping us in contact with Singapore; and my friend, Jothie Rajah, for her help on drafts of this book.

There is, finally, my wife, Siow Jin Hua, for our life together in America.

part one
dreams of america

an introduction to customs

I WAS BORN AMERICAN. Not in the country itself, but in its shadow. Coca-Cola and jeans were always in, no matter how the governments of Singapore and of Asia railed against "yellow" culture in the 1960s and 1970s, or "decadent" Western values. By my late teens, McDonald's and other fast-food joints were the hangouts; others younger than I were born into that urban landscape and cannot imagine life without them. In our mindscapes, TV and movies made us visualise new places and situations. They taught us new words, ways of speaking and dressing, new lifestyles. Sex, drugs and rock-n-roll were part of it; the most censurable part. Harder to keep out (if anyone wanted to) were money, big business and cities with skyscrapers, cars and shopping malls, TV, movies and stars, consumer culture. The whole American cult.

It did not matter that Singapore was almost exactly halfway across the world. America, like a blockbuster movie, was projected in every neighbourhood, big-screen. Through the small screen, the TV, it beamed into every living room. Most of us did not mind what other developing countries complained of as cultural imperialism. American multi-national companies with large investments and large payrolls were always welcome in Singapore, even in the 1960s and 1970s when other developing countries kept them out or confiscated their properties. An American armed presence was seen not as a sign of foreign domination but as a cornerstone of peace, well beyond the Vietnam war. No matter that in big ways – in the language we use at home, among ourselves, in religion, in race – many Singaporeans remain Asian. Or that the English were our original colonisers, with a lingering influence in history and education. Even if we did not eat apple pie, salute the Stars-n-Stripes and have the American accent, there was something we liked in it all, the all-Americanness of it. My family was no exception.

In 1971, my father was awarded an Eisenhower fellowship. He toured the country almost from coast to coast, my mother accompanying him for several months. In most places, the people organising the fellowship arranged for them to stay with Americans in their homes, to get to meet real people, outside hotels and the tourist industry. My parents dined at the Windows of the World, astride what then was the world's tallest building. They met Wall Street bankers, Washington big-wigs, Californian business executives, Sun Belt retirees, Mid-West farmers. When they came back, America returned with them. My mother's favourite city in the world was

New Orleans. My father read Kissinger's memoirs, Schlesinger on the New Deal and Sorenson's recollection of Kennedy. I saw their snapshots, read their books, heard their tales of new friends, broad horizons and good times. *Go West, young man.*

For me and so many others in Asia, America was the highway to the future, the epitome of success, the stuff of modern dreams. Singapore – home for MNCs, fast-food joints and malls – was travelling that highway, dreaming those dreams. It was only a matter of time, with growing affluence and cheaper airfares, that I, like so many Singaporeans and other Asians, went to visit America, first-hand. Some went as tourists. Many others as students, making America one of the top destinations for Singaporeans seeking tertiary education. Some – especially in the 1980s – as immigrants. Crossing the Pacific became as simple as taking a bus to JB. And when we went to America, it was not as strangers. We tested, intentionally or otherwise, the land of our dreams against its reality.

Asians are increasing in number and profile in America, especially on the West Coast. They have their own businesses. Growing numbers have entered the ranks of professionals in computing, law, accounting, engineering and even classical music. In some prestigious universitiess like Berkeley in California, they feature in disproportionately large numbers. Yo-Yo Ma, the cellist; the architect, I.M. Pei; Vinod Kholsa, co-founder of Sun Microsystems; writers Amy Tan and Bhatah Mukherjee; actors and playwrights like David Hwang; Aids researcher and *Time* magazine Man of the Year in 1996, David Ho; Gary

Locke, the governor of Washington State; Jerry Yang, the founder of the Yahoo! Internet search engine; new-age guru Depak Chopra: these are the community's icons. The computer programmer, the small business-man and grocery-store owner, the engineer, scientist: these are the community's typical profile. Asians are now regarded as a model minority.

But Asian-Americans have not had success in all sectors of society. They have not been a significant factor in politics. At the national level, there is only one Asian-American Congressman who is of Korean ancestry. On the West Coast, with millions of Asians, no state-elected office was won by an Asian until the recent election of Governor Locke. Only the state of Hawaii, halfway across the Pacific Ocean and where the majority are of Asian origin, witnesses a significant presence.

Nor have all types of Asians been successful in their claim to the American dream. Some sub-groups are unable to cope and remain predominately on welfare. Among the Indo-Chinese refugees, as many as one in three is unemployed and living off welfare. The Hmong from Cambodia, for example, are largely a rural people without formal education or proficiency in English. Brought to America in the wake of the Vietnam war, many were settled in peaceful, small Mid-Western towns. But their economic weakness and their cultural and linguistic insularity have worn out their welcome quickly. Divisions and tensions with the predominately White population in these areas have grown.

Even those who have done well find that success is not a shield. Being a model minority can mean Asians are targets. In the LA riots of 1992, the primary target of Black anger was not the Whites nor the police officers who beat up Rodney King; it was the Asian grocery stores and small businesses. In some universities, Asians have been so successful in getting admitted that they are no longer entitled to preferential treatment as a minority. Instead, there is talk of putting a cap to their numbers to make space for other minority races and prevent the Whites from being displaced. Among many Americans of other colours, there is an ambivalence towards Asians.

The fluctuation between welcome and xenophobia is not new. In the 19th century, Asian migration to California, known as "the Gold Mountain", soared. Tens of thousands of Asians, mainly Chinese, were imported as labourers to build roads and the railway system in what was called the "pig trade". By 1880, there were about 105,000 Chinese in America, mainly on the West Coast. As the White population in the region expanded, so did prejudice and antipathy against the Chinese. Their import was controlled and their women excluded, so they could not settle. In 1882, Congress barred further immigration with the Chinese Exclusion Act.

Japanese then took up this slack. They entered the fabled land of California as craftsmen, market gardeners, houseboys, fishermen. Like the Chinese, they were treated as transients, not immigrants. They could not own property. Even American-born Japanese were excluded from the State school systems. They and other "Orientals" were held to be inadmissible for citizenship. In World War II, although many had been in America for generations and were by then citizens, Japanese-Americans in California had their homes and possessions taken from them. They were interned for the duration of the war. In cases such as Korematsu, that sought to have such laws declared illegal for racism, the US Supreme Court, the champion of liberty, approved such laws as constitutional.

The history of Asians in America differs from the experience of European migrants. They too came in pursuit of utopia, to escape famine and oppression – from the first English pilgrim settlers to successive waves of Irish, Polish, and Italian. They too faced initial discrimination. But Americans originally of European stock have since been allowed to fit into the White mainstream. Asians have not.

In the days before I left for America, my friends and I sat in a food court of a shopping arcade on Orchard Road, exchanging stories about America. Eddie had been there for ten years, living on both coasts. Studying mainly, but also working a bit and bumming, growing his hair in a pony-tail, falling in love with a series of American girls. Pin had adored New York and its art galleries. I had my own journeys too, visiting thrice since 1989, seeing both coasts, dropping in on Texas and making extended stays in the Mid-West as a fellow at the International Writing Program of the University of Iowa. Everyone there had been, for some time and for some reason, to America.

No problem, my friends assured me. Sure to fit in. There would be the LA airport, exactly as seen in a thousand movies and TV programmes. There would be crowded highways and sprawling, plush suburbs. Tall, large men – tough and intelligent. Glamourous, rich blonde women. The polished MTV teenagers who both inspire and are inspired by Beverly Hills 90210. The coast and the Californian sun. New York, like a Woody Allen setting. Life would be TV, soap opera, movie.

My friends and I drank *tau hwey chui* – that particularly Asian drink of soya bean milk. But the Orchard Road shopping arcade and food court – in concept, neon signs, marble floors and plastic trays – was already a part of America, right here in Singapore. And we drank from disposable cups, emblazoned in red and white, "Coca-Cola". With that heady mix of Asian and American, home and foreign, we toasted my departure. Between all that I had read, heard, seen, arriving in America would be more of a homecoming. Or so I thought. Reality has a way of intruding into dreams, American or otherwise.

❖

The arrival hall at LA resounded with different accents and languages – Spanish, Japanese, Chinese and East European. Tourists, businessmen and -women, students and immigrants: we all waited in snaking queues, dwarfed by tall columns. The Americans returning passed through a different channel, quickly and confidently. Once fellow passengers on the plane, they no longer looked at us. We were aliens. That is the official categorisation of those who are neither American citizens nor permanent residents: "aliens". The word suggests people from a different world, wholly different and perhaps dangerous. That is how we were treated.

We waited, small figures in a large hall. The long lines moved slowly. Many felt both expectant and anxious. Expectant because they waited to enter the US, much as the Spanish Conquistadors once sought El Dorado. Anxious because, before entering this paradise, aliens faced the grand inquisition by US Immigration and Customs authorities.

From among us aliens, a fair, silver-haired woman went up to the tall desk. She showed her passport and papers and then the officer, an African-American, spoke to her. She looked back, blankly. He repeated himself. Very loudly. Very slowly. It was to no avail. He spoke only English. She, a Mexican, knew only Spanish. For a while, until a bilingual officer came, I found myself translating between them, finding an unexpected use for the limited vocabulary I picked up while travelling in South America some years ago. What they made of a Chinese Singaporean speaking English and Spanish, I had no idea.

Mrs Ramirez said she would be met by her daughter, who held a Green Card, that vital document that hundreds of thousands in the world outside America aspire to. She intended to stay for a month or so. I translated. The immigration man scowled and asked gruffly for a permanent address. Also for a return ticket as proof that she could return to Mexico. She looked across to me quizzically and scowled at him. Mrs Ramirez might not have understood the officer's English but the gruff suspicion of his questions was apparent. A return air-ticket, I interpreted, could she show one? Mrs Ramirez dug into her handbag and produced it like a golden key. She suddenly smiled and offered a letter from her daughter, eager to please, obsequious. There is no need, the officer muttered. Then the translator came and I returned to the queue of aliens. The immigration officer continued thumbing through the woman's passport. A few more questions were asked. Then, he stamped the passport and waved her through: his satisfaction as mysterious as the earlier doubt.

When my turn came, my red Singaporean passport passed muster. So did my language. My J–I visa was stamped and the white form completed. I was instructed to keep one form in my passport until I left America and to give another form to the institution that I was going to. I nodded. Exit and entry points show off their petty jealousies in guarding the dividing lines between states, often imaginary lines. Bureaucracies, American or otherwise, have similar rituals. But there was more ahead, the matter of clearing customs. Here my Singaporean passport did not reassure. I was not waved through. I was directed, with all my luggage, to an additional inspection line. There, I was quizzed if my bags contained food, fruits or agricultural products. I said no. But the bags were still tediously opened and inspected. Everyone else in the line was also Asian. Perhaps we had a reputation for smuggling exotic foodstuffs. If so, that day it was justified.

Someone in front was found with contraband – a large packet of dried mushrooms. They were immediately confiscated. The mushroom smuggler was wearing a polo shirt and navy blazer with shiny gold buttons. Half-hidden in his hands was an American passport. He stammered out an excuse in an American accent. The customs officer just shook his head and looked towards the next persons in the queue: us. What did they think of us, cross-Pacific smugglers? Why were we Asians bringing food into the land of plenty? We had thought of bringing in *belachan*. Would that, with its strong smell (or worse, durian), have resulted in deportation?

Cleared through at last, we re-packed and re-boarded, for the final leg of our journey. Half a day later, we had crossed the continent from California to New England, reversing the westward journey that the Americans took. We stood at the baggage carousel at Boston's Logan Airport. We had four bulging, over-sized bags. For this journey, unlike our past travels, Jin Hua and I had packed heavily. We carried everything we thought we might need from a home an ocean away: clothes from a different climate, books studying a different mind-set and milieu, even a wok for our own type of cooking. While we waited, our friends arrived.

Ken was Chinese, from Malaysia, a friend from old days in Singapore. He had been in North America since he was 19, returning only to do his Master's at the National University of Singapore. Geulf was where he had started, an isolated spot in Canada that Ken ironically dubbed "the centre of the world". He then studied in Miami and Oregon before moving to take up a post-graduate position in Boston. And so he had moved from the centre of the continent to cities on almost every coast: the South, Pacific Northwest and the New England East Coast. Along the journey, he met Danna, the American blonde who had become his wife in the last year.

We had met them last in Singapore some six months before. We were then thinking of coming to America but were not settled on exactly where to go. We had called long-distance when we knew it would be in the Boston area, where Ken and Danna lived. And so they met us at the airport. At the baggage carousel, we exchanged greetings and news of events in Singapore and the USA, all the comings and goings of our lives and those of our friends on the shrinking globe.

The luggage finally came and we left, because of the size of the bags, in two cars. Ken and Danna had arranged to take us to our other friends who lived in the city, a Singaporean couple with whom we would stay until we found a new home. We drove off from the airport, putting the experience of arrival behind us.

There was a highway. It took us through grey outlying neighbourhoods and sprawling malls, past the core of Boston with its glassy skyscrapers, and out again, across a river, into the smaller town with narrow rows of houses. The geography was at once strange and yet familiar.

We stopped at a house on a dark street and rang the doorbell. The door opened after some minutes to reveal Karen, a good friend but someone we had not seen for almost a year, since she went to America. As she welcomed us, Ken and Danna said their goodbyes. They would come back the next day, they promised, to talk and take us around the town. Karen took us upstairs to meet Linus, her husband. How was the flight? How was going through Immigration and Customs?

Karen told us her horror stories of transit and arrival. We recounted ours. "That's the problem," she said. "Immigration's okay if you have the right visa and forms.

What always causes you problems is Customs." I nodded: it was a matter of customs.

Singaporeans know America: this is partly true. Yet there are some things we do not know. America has a special openness to novelty and change. The historian Daniel Boorstein observed that it interacts "on the verge" between the known and unknown, what it is and what it is becoming – whether in geography, politics, technology or generational change.

"When we (Americans) encounter something different," Boorstein said, "we become aware that things can be different, our appetite is whetted for novelty and its charms." Allied to this, the historian suggested that Americans "in the face of the different and unfamiliar also, we, the similar, lean on one another . . . to reassure one another." These different tendencies are sometimes contradictory and at other times, complementary.

They create the apparent uniformity of skyscrapers, malls, highways and suburbs; the face of American culture that is projected through the TV. But, beneath that is a greater complexity. Between and beyond New York and Los Angeles, the usual depictions of the mass media, there is something different. The Mid-West and the South, the mountains and the coasts, the small towns and rural communities: regions differ – not only in geography, but also in culture, people, industry, lifestyle, past and future, needs and aims. People are different, as you might expect in a country where individuality and diversity seem sacrosanct. Not all the men are cowboys. Not all the women are blonde or dress in designer clothes. Like most clichés and common wisdom, they are partly true. But only partly. The picture of America that is broadcast across the world, across the Pacific, is too simple. By reason of its character, its size and history, there is the unexpected and less known in America. There is variety and complexity.

The Spanish-speaking Mrs Ramirez comes from a world that – in some ways – is further from the English-speaking USA than I am, even if she is from neighbouring Mexico. Yet, with or without her daughter, she will easily fit into neighbourhoods where Spanish prevails, whether among illegal immigrants or in the increasingly Hispanic Southwest and Florida.

The Asian mushroom smuggler can be American, perhaps an accountant, perhaps a grocery store owner. He, like many Asians, will have found a home in America – whether in Chinatown and ethnic enclaves, or in more comfortable upper-middle-class suburbia. Both of them – although stalled at the process of entry by language or prohibited mushrooms – have a home here. They are not aliens. I am.

Later, unpacked and relaxing in our friends' new home, from the long flight and queue, I drank a toast to knowing more about America. The toast was not made with Californian wine or Coke, but by drinking soya bean milk – just as I had in Singapore, with other friends, a world away. It had an assuring taste, having been bought fresh from a Chinatown store. And it was made in the USA. It was no surprise to learn that America was the world's largest producer of soya beans. That was part of the complexity of America, and of being an alien Asian in the country.

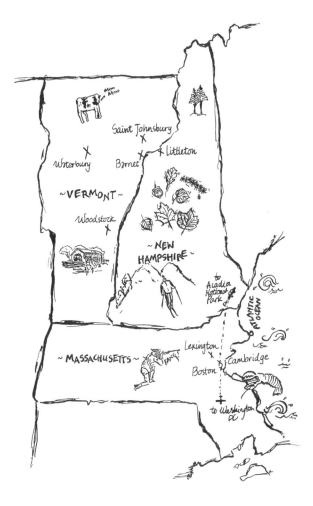

necessities
of life

CAMBRIDGE, Massachusetts is a small but increasingly crowded town. It is home to a number of universities, including perhaps the best known in America: Harvard. The focus of the town is Harvard Square, just outside the gates of the university, beyond the famous Yard with its ivy-covered buildings and domed steeples. The Square is not, however, a haven of scholarly quiet. It thrives and bustles with buskers, professors, bums and doctoral candidates, tourists and undergrads. There are bookstores like the Harvard Book Store and Wordsworth, bagel shops and bad Chinese restaurants. There is the subway entrance and Out of Town Tickets, an encyclopedic magazine and newspaper shop with everything from the *New York Times* to Spanish dailies, from the *New Republic* to porn mags. Around the Square, there are shops like the Gap, Body Shop, Tower Records and the ridiculously overpriced university cooperative, called the Coop. At the centre, there is an open-air café – Euro-style but part of an American chain – where, beneath the trees, self-proclaimed chess experts take on all-comers for $2 a game. Intellectualism, yuppie ambition, street life and entertainment mix to make a unique place.

There are very few who can claim to be a native. Almost everyone comes to Cambridge for a few years and then moves on. Everyone is from somewhere else, whether from another state in the USA or another country. No one belongs here, so everyone – including me – does. We are all citizens of Harvard Square. I felt that from the first time we visited the Square.

"Hey, man. How ya doin'?" The voice was a song without music, a rap. He was a tall African-American in jeans and boots, both badly scuffed, a plain T-shirt and – even in the summer heat – a cap. "Hi, you're looking good. Real good. You got your woman and the day is treating you good, right?" He held out a newspaper. He smiled, as my pace slowed. "Buy one. Help the homeless. *Spare Change* is about the homeless, by the homeless."

"Spare Change?"

"Yeah, man. That's the name of this newspaper. It's written about the homeless, by the homeless."

"How much is it?"

"One dollar. Just one dollar. For that you get some-thing to read, and you help the homeless help them-selves."

I looked around the Square. At almost every corner, where there wasn't a busker playing music, there was someone with a sign and a cup, or a box, asking for money. A hand-out, to use an American term. Spare change: I dug into my pockets and gave him a dollar. "You have a wonderful day, now. Welcome to Harvard." He smiled at us briefly. Then it was on to the next person who came along.

Almost every day, for as long as I lived in Cambridge, I would come to the Square. I regularly went to the Algiers coffee shop on Brattle Street, with its faux Moroccan decor of Muslim design and authentic, thick coffee. I haunted the bookstores; sometimes Wordsworth, near the Algiers, but most often the Harvard Book Store, with its wide reach of literary and intellectual titles and its remainder section, where you could buy hardbacks for less than $5. Most of the time, I went alone because there was little need for company if there were books and a good cup of coffee.

At other times, I would go with my classmates to the Algiers, to sit in the open air Au Bon Pain. There we would chat idly or talk about what we were studying and experiencing at Harvard. Events and ideas swirled around us at those cafés, at the Square, just outside Harvard Yard. We talked with almost endless enthusiasm about what these might mean to us and the different societies we had come from. I enjoyed these talks, those times. But, even then, I felt that this was something to do for just the limited time I was there. These were the conversations of those who visited and enjoyed their visit, but belonged elsewhere, to which they would take something back.

Each month, I would stop to buy a copy of *Spare Change*. The homeless would be there in almost all weather, right through summer and fall, some even when the sun had gone and the January snow was on the ground. They too were citizens of Harvard Square; they belonged there more than I did. Not least, this tall man with his good-humoured banter and folded newsletters. Each month, I always bought *Spare Change* from him. He would always be lively, have something to say. He would never know my name and I would not ask his. But I always thought of him as "Harvie", because he was the first person to welcome me to Harvard Square.

Beyond the Square, going past the John F. Kennedy School of Government, it is an easy walk to the Charles River, with its green banks and paths for walking or cycling. There is the Wicks pedestrian bridge. There are Harvard's boat houses from which the typical, photo-genic rowing skulls are launched. Nearby, there is more ivy-covered housing for the thousands of undergrads. Further east, Boston can be seen just across the water: its skyscrapers and the sprawl of buildings. Cambridge is close enough to have access to all the big city conven-iences and culture. Yet it remains sufficiently removed to escape the full brunt of the urban poverty and crime that afflict so many American cities. Cambridge claims the title as the country's capital for stolen bicycles – the students' prime mode of transport – but it is still a desirable place to live in America. And, for us, the most convenient. Our plans were that I would attend the law school, north of the Square, while Jin Hua would cross the river to go to university in Boston.

We started searching for a home. We scanned the newspapers and the lists of available apartments at the university housing office. There was a great demand for rentals, given the influx of students and researchers at Harvard, and limited supply in relatively small Cambridge. So our search went on for days, stretching into weeks. Nothing seemed both affordable and suitable. The Singaporean friends we were staying with, Karen and Linus, were invaluable in our search.

Having come a year before us, Karen sat us down with a map of Cambridge to spell out where things were. She offered helpful advice on the ins and outs, on the ways of getting things done in this foreign environment, even the use of her car. With her help, we learnt our way around, not just about the main streets but also about the supermarkets, the places for good coffee, sandwiches, stationery and warm clothes. Karen's help seemed an eerie echo of clan associations in Singapore or Chinatown: how those immigrants who first came assisted late-comers who hailed from the same village or claimed the same surname. Coincidentally, Karen and I were both Tays.

The Kohs lived in Central Square and it was the first neighbourhood we came to know in Cambridge. It is funky, just one stop from Harvard on the Red Line underground train, and gritty. There were donut shops and low-price convenience stores. There was one Chinese restaurant and a few Asian faces, but many more were African- and Hispanic-Americans. It seemed more like New York than New England. The Kohs' house was in a terrace row of those tall but narrow buildings that typify parts of older cities. Their unit on the corner had however been re-done. There were sky lights and higher ceilings, sand-coloured wooden floors, a hi-tech kitchen and a black jacuzzi-bathtub in the main bathroom. It was not so different from the apartment they used to have in Singapore, an ultra-modern condominium just off Orchard Road. The similarity was compounded by the furniture. Chairs, dining table, shelving unit and desk: all this and more had come with them from Singapore.

"We had to do something with our furniture after we sold our old place," Karen explained. "So we just put everything into a container and shipped it over. The whole house fit into one container. It was pretty easy, easier than having to look for furniture again."

Karen told us how they had found the house. They saw it the day after they arrived in Cambridge, the first place they viewed – then still under renovation. They met the owners and, after she had talked to the wife for a while, Linus struck a deal with the husband. Financing was unnecessary since, having sold their flat in Singapore for a handsome profit, they paid in cash. Within a week, they had moved in, making do until the furniture arrived and all the work on the house was finished. They did not regret the decision, however quickly taken. But other possibilities had arisen. There were opportunities that might take Linus, a banker, to London. There were also dangers.

"It's not that safe here," Karen confessed in a low voice. "Not as safe as back home. We've been thinking of moving out to the suburbs so the kids will have more green spaces. There are better, safer areas. But here," she sighed, "at least the police station is right across the street."

After a week or so, we began to consider buying a place as the Kohs had. It seemed to make sense, given the strong Singapore dollar, and the Singaporean hunger to invest rather than rent. For that, we engaged a housing agent. Lisa was delighted to have us. She was a big woman with a lots of curly blonde hair. She wore a skirt suit with large, padded shoulders, and drove a blue Peugeot. Her accent was slightly southern, betraying a Texan origin. She asked where we were from. But when we replied, "Singapore," she only smiled blankly and said that she had just helped a Japanese couple secure their home. "I showed it to them and they just loved it. Bought it straightaway. I have an idea of what Asians like. And you Asians have money, I know."

In the car, she gave us a brochure, listing hundreds of places that were available, either in Cambridge or the adjacent township of Sommerville, which is only two or three streets from the university, divided by an imaginary line along Beacon Street. Housing there is cheaper but, with too many streets and houses in bad condition, it is known as "slummer-ville". Many places there were dumps, Lisa warned us, some had been on sale for more than a year without success. Lisa reassured us that she would guide us through a selection of the best in our price range. In a week, we looked at over 30 properties, with her or on our own. Beyond the list she gave us, we followed up on advertisements in the newspapers or posted on supermarket noticeboards.

One of the first places we saw in Cambridge was furnished with antiques and rich carpets. A tidy apartment in a brick building, close to streets with pure white houses and neat, trimmed lawns. We were attracted but the owner declined us as tenants, preferring a visiting

English professor, even if our money was the same colour. At the next place we inspected, across Beacon Street's invisible boundary, in Sommerville, the whole interior was thickly painted a chocolate brown. In the middle of a hot afternoon, the out-going occupant stood at the countertop in the small kitchenette. He was shirtless and spoke Spanish to a friend while chopping a raw chicken with a thick blade. He looked up blankly at us when we walked in. Then the blade cut through the chicken to the already broken and stained formica of the countertop, leaving another layer of grease and blood. Just outside, large trailers rumbled past. We declined the tenancy.

Another place Lisa took us to was in East Cambridge. The apartment was done up with black and white tiles in the kitchen, track lighting and walls splashed with colour. It was yuppie chic, like something out of a home decoration magazine.

"This house is something special," Lisa gushed. "The owners really loved it. They spent a lot of money doing it up. They didn't want to leave."

"Why did they?" Jin asked.

"The lights come with it," Lisa went on. "And if you like the furniture, they're willing to sell it too. Isn't the kitchen just great?"

"We're a bit concerned about the neighbourhood," Jin said.

"Oh, this is quite a good area, really. There's a park at the corner, and in the evenings when I drive home, I can see all the kids from the neighbourhood there. Why don't you go see for yourself?"

We went down the narrow, curving stairs. The house looked good from the outside too. It was made from wooden slats, like most houses in Cambridge. The paint was in good condition and the grass in the front and side yards was cut, well kempt. The house stood neat and yuppie-like. But, down to the corner, the rest of the street was a row of run-down houses. Some had junk left out in their porches and front gardens. Others had rusted gutters and peeling paint. Down at the corner, there was a liquor store with broken windows. Two men were sitting and drinking at the curb side, in the middle of the day.

Jin and I walked down the street. An old Black woman was standing on the porch of a house, leaning with one arm against a wooden pillar that was thick with dark, green paint. Through her glasses, she stared out at us as we passed. I nodded, trying to be neighbourly since I was trying out the neighbourhood, but she just turned away. We walked to the corner. The sidewalk broadened. There was a wooden bench, carved with explicit graffiti about a person named Robin. There were a few flowering bushes and the pavement was punched through in places to let scraggly grass and some weeds poke through. There was a strong smell. Perhaps ammonia, possibly urine. The park bench faced the liquor store across the street. This, Jin Hua said, was what Lisa had meant by a "park", not the grassy space and playground the word evoked for me. We walked back to the house and Lisa. "Think about it," she advised. "It's a good buy."

As we headed back to Harvard Square in her European-made car, she chattered on about other possibilities. Out the windows, we saw – slowly, now – the patchwork of neighbourhoods in the city. Some green with lawns and trees, others brown with rust and rotten wood panels; some with Persian carpets, others greasy; some rich, many poor.

❖

Our hosts, the Kohs, had come to Cambridge a year or so before us. Karen had been offered a place to do her Master's in tax policy at the John F. Kennedy school, part of Harvard University. Linus, who already had an MBA from the well-known Sloan school at MIT, initially helped settle the three children into school and then found a job with a Boston bank. After their first year, Karen decided to stay on to do some research and pursue a doctorate while Linus headed a department in the bank. They were well settled, with a BMW and an Audi, a golf club membership, a good Montessori school for the kids, part-time help to clean the house and keep an eye on the children after school.

But they continued to think of Singapore as home. Karen cooked all the local dishes they missed, with ingredients found in Chinatown supermarkets. They spoke English with a recognisable Singaporean accent with us even if, when speaking with others, they would shift to a slightly more American style. They fought a losing battle to keep their children from using more and more American words and pronunciations, then arranged for them to have Mandarin tuition. They kept in close contact with their families back home, chalking up high international phone bills, and returning for a long stay in the summer. The Kohs, like so many Singaporeans and other Asians, seemed to stand at some place between fitting into America and looking back, over their shoulders, across the Pacific, homewards.

They came to represent, in my mind, the new Singaporean living abroad: with education and money to afford more than scruffy, poor neighbourhoods that most newcomers make do with when they arrive. They had no stated intention of permanently leaving Singapore. There was, however, the possibility of staying abroad for prolonged periods. A prospect that was real, even if seldom discussed.

The Kohs were a long way from Chinatown. That was, however, where Karen took us one afternoon, to go shopping for provisions. Boston's Chinatown is a grimy place, right next to the red-light district known as the Combat Zone. Chinatowns across America are notorious for their squalor and what White Americans think of as arcane "Oriental" ways. Not good or safe areas, unless recently refurbished. They are, after all, where the Chinese first settled when they got off the boat, penniless.

In some cities, it was the only section in which Chinese were allowed to settle because other city areas had White-only zoning laws. With the repeal of such laws and growing affluence, many original denizens of Chinatown have since moved out to nicer, cleaner places. Chinatowns have, however, continued, hosting new waves of arrivals and a wider range of Asians, especially the Indo-Chinese. But even if Asians have escaped Chinatown, as Karen had, they must also return – at least for provisions that make up food for the Asian stomach and soul.

The pot-holed streets of Chinatown were streaked with dirt. The air on a warm afternoon was heavy. Everything smelt. Cantonese and other dialects, not American-twanged English, could be heard. Karen, tall and stylish in an off-white, linen outfit, seemed out of place in every aspect except race and culinary preference.

We shopped for the essential provisions. They had everything: chilli and other sauces and *bok choy*, fresh *kway chap* and *char siew pau* made for the microwave, the *tau hwei chui* I had drunk that first night, even frozen durian. The aisles were crammed and narrow compared to the bright airy spaces of the typical American supermarket. The trolleys were smaller. All of them had bad wheels. There were familiar brands like Yeo's and Amoy Canning. There were mysterious packages and tins that I had never seen and knew nothing about, from Vietnam, China and other parts of Asia.

Walking along the aisles, I overheard a young American couple, the only Whites in the entire place.

"You see," the man said, loudly, excitedly to the woman, "I told you. This is where they all shop. Look at the stuff."

"It's so different," she replied, excited too.

"And so cheap. No wonder they can get by with so little money."

"But do you know what this is?" the woman asked, holding up a vacuum-sealed package with dark contents.

"No," the man admitted, somewhat crestfallen. "But

I love Asian food. And I want to buy some stuff and try to cook it at home."

"Sure." The reply was slightly doubtful. "If you know what you're buying."

"Ask someone," he finished, brightly.

They walked ahead, holding up the packet like an alien specimen. The woman tried an old Chinese lady in an embroidered, slightly grubby sweater. The response came in Cantonese, uncomprehending and unhelpful. Then we moved near them and they asked Karen. They repeated the question; the American woman, speaking slowly and loudly, pointed repeatedly to the package. Karen paused and looked at the package. The wording was in Thai or Vietnamese, a script that was incomprehensible to us. She shrugged and suggested they ask at the cashier. From their faces, I detected surprise that the reply was in crisp, grammatical English. More, there was surprise that Karen, an Asian, did not know what this Asian product was.

Karen did not tell them she was an English-speaking Singaporean and a Harvard grad, and about our Cold Storage supermarkets. She did not try to educate them about the many different languages and cuisines in Asia. She wheeled the trolley ahead to her next purchase, leaving the couple to their exoticism. We were in Chinatown after all. Here, I realised, to White eyes, Singaporeans, Malaysians, Chinese, Koreans, Japanese, Thais, Vietnamese, Burmese, all of us Asians, were the same.

❖

Back in Cambridge, we finally found a home. It was 32 Winslow Street, about 20 minutes' walk from the law school and Harvard Square; on the other side of the Square from the Kohs. It was a one-bedroom ground-floor flat, one of four apartments in a big clapboard white house on a dead-end street. It was pleasant, with a large living and dining area, new wooden floors, a modern kitchen and heating system. But the nicest part of the place was the porch that opened out onto a garden. A yard, to use the American term. Big enough to make you sweat mowing the grass and raking the leaves. Big enough to stretch your legs and potter around with the flowers that grew along the fence. For a picnic or BBQ, in spring and summer. In the coming winter, to hold the snow, pristine white; inviolable when all the city streets had turned a slushy brown.

The yard was not ours exclusively; the four apartment shared it. So here, in the house on a quiet street, with a porch that faced a communal yard, we would come to know Americans as neighbours. There were John and Hilary Hopkins, an active and adventurous couple in their late 50s, in their second marriage, who had a canoe that they paddled in the river come summer. In the apartment directly above us was Helen, a computer programmer, a gaunt woman with thin lips which hardly ever stretched into a smile. In the last apartment, a woman named Anita who, at about 70, spent half the year in Paris and was seldom seen. In the next house, on our side of the street, were Edna and Barbara, two sisters nearly 70, both with hair gone completely white but a steady step and voice. We would come to know each of them, not well, but with the easy exchanges and brief conversations that mark acquaintances in America.

These things and many others that come with settling into a new home were, however, still ahead of us. First, we had to meet the landlords. It was not enough that they were willing to let the premises at a certain price, and we were prepared to rent it. The estate agent told us they would like to meet us, to see whom they were entrusting their property to. I could only agree and hope there would be no racial prejudice.

Richard was a tall, balding White American, a lawyer. He was formal when we first met. We talked about security deposits and when we would vacate the place. They planned to sell the apartment, he explained, and to show it in good condition, he must ensure that it was well up-kept by the tenant. Graduate students generally did not have a good reputation for that. Asians, moreover, had a reputation for the smell and mess of Chinatown. He did not say that and did not have to. It seemed we would not get the place after all.

But stereotypes can help as much as hurt. We discovered that his wife was from Boston University, where Jin Hua studied. Moreover, Richard himself was from Harvard, the same law school I would be attending. We shared alma maters. Perhaps the key point, however, was to portray ourselves as a particular type of Asian. We complained about the slummy apartments we had seen and the mess that students – mainly American – had left behind. We expressed disdain for loud and messy parties. Jin Hua played the role of dutiful Asian wife and home-maker. In the empty apartment, she talked about the possibilities of curtains and paintings. Looking out at the garden, she expressed an interest in putting in more flowers. These things were true but the context changed their truth. They were now details that went towards distinguishing us from the Chinatown-type of Asian. We were instead the more monied and house-proud new Asian. One stereotype was exchanged for another. This time, however, to our benefit. Richard and I shook hands and, being lawyers, discussed the contract details. The apartment was ours.

We would soon accumulate a table to work on, an art deco bed, a dresser, and a dining table and chairs borrowed from our friends, Ken and Danna: all the paraphernalia of a normal life, the things that make an empty space a home. Jin Hua would find the necessary things and touches from garage sales, that particularly American institution, where everything from books to bathroom mats to beds can be bought; from discount stores; and from antique dealers.

The first thing Jin Hua spotted was an old travelling trunk. It was something she had always wanted. It was being sold for a modest price in a neighbouring town, some 20 minutes away. The house stood on a hill, surrounded by greenery. The seller was a woman in her 60s, getting rid of an heirloom from her mother's time because she needed the storage space. We had a short but agreeable conversation. She asked where we were from, what we were doing, and told us her husband also went to the same law school, decades ago. We agreed on a price and then I heaved the enormous if elegant object onto a trolley. But it would not fit into the trunk of our rented car.

"I'll help you," the woman volunteered. "Where do you live?" We told her and she knew the place. It was not too far. With that, we put the trunk into their station wagon, and she and her husband followed us to our house. There, I unloaded it and thanked them. But there weren't even cups to offer them some coffee. Never mind, the couple smiled as they left. We waved and went back into the apartment, and closed the door. Except for a futon bed, the trunk was our first piece of furniture. It spoke of travel, but it also made the place our home. The unexpected help from this American couple whom we would never meet again was our first house-warming present.

There must have been many more houses like ours in Cambridge. Thousands descend on the town each year as the new school term approaches. And, in many more, across the country, people must have been starting in a new place. Not just foreigners, aliens, but also Americans who move from one city to another, for studies, job, spouse or just to start over in a new place.

Not everyone chooses the fast pace of New York, Washington DC or LA, with their attendant stresses and dangers. Some may end up in greener and safer suburbs and towns like Cambridge, within commuting distance of big cities. Others opt for secondary cities, like Seattle – still big, but not a megapolis. Still others decide on a more rustic life in smaller towns and villages, which – although we did not know it then – we too would experience.

Those are the possibilities in America. Beyond the safe, mainly White suburbs and well-established, richer neighbourhoods, there are some areas where almost everyone is Black (or African-American, as they are now called). Others, where everyone speaks Spanish. And there are Chinatowns too.

For the majority, those who have some means, America offers choice and freedom in making a home, to have a place of your own. There are many more who rent because they cannot afford more, and just an illness or losing their jobs can leave them in the streets. There are also the homeless — like Harvie of Harvard Square.

In our new home, on a dead-end street in Cambridge, we locked the doors and windows. Even if it was still unfurnished except for a futon and a travelling trunk, we slept easily from the first night.

❖

I bought the American dream. Or, at least, a major part of it: a car. In America, a car means success and freedom. It represents middle-class purchasing power and the right to get up and hit the road, to go anywhere. When Americans talk about the pursuit of happiness, that pursuit is by car. With the windows down and the radio blasting too.

That is the legend of the road. Almost all Americans can regale you with stories from a trip they've taken on the highways, whether with their family or buddies. Most of the time is spent in the car. They sing songs — whether on tape, radio or sing-alongs in the vein of "1,000 bottles

sea". You pass through four time zones. You pass

of beer on the wall". They eat in roadside diners and stay overnight in motels. They stop for gas and to use the john. They hop out to visit some sight or museum for a few minutes. Then they move on. The country stretches from New York to San Francisco – "from sea to shining sea". You pass through four time zones. You pass through states where 12 hours of driving brings nothing but corn fields. Our American friend Danna told us about her road trip.

"I was leaving Oregon to join Ken here in Boston. I sold off most of the furniture in a garage sale. Whatever else I had, I put into a rented U-haul truck and headed east. I left that same evening. There were three of us. Made it from Portland to Boston in just about three days. That was about as fast as we could do it. We didn't stop anywhere except to get some food and use the toilets. We split the driving between us, kept going day and night by shifts, with one person taking the wheel and another to keep company, while the third caught a nap in the back seat.

"I don't remember much. But there was a lot we passed that was just fields and fields of corn and wheat. Flat and bare. With just the road running through it all. This is a big country. The trip made me realise that."

The American highway system stretches from coast to coast, traversing every sort of terrain: swamps, rivers as wide as seas, mountain ranges and deserts. To exist is to drive – especially since the public transport system in most places is almost non-existent. Consequently, everyone in America seems to have a car, whether a shiny new Beemer or a beat-up rusting hulk. To make it affordable, American industry created the first mass-produced car, the Ford model T, and still churns out new models every year. The car is a consumer item, cheap. You can get something that moves for as little as $500. The cheapest new car, a Yugo, is about $4,000. Even a Merc 190 starts at about $20,000. The situation in Singapore, with taxes and COEs, is very different. But perhaps envy is not completely deserved. The American legend of the road has a less mythic reality.

"You've got to get some sort of safety device, maybe a steering lock," Ken counselled when we bought our car. "So if they break into the car, they can't drive it away. If you have an anti-theft device, you get a discount on insurance. Otherwise, the rates are high. Car theft," he admitted the obvious, "happens."

Alarmed myself, I sought anti-theft devices for my car; electronic gadgetry that short-circuits the ignition until a secret number is punched in. The Club was what Ken used. It was a heavy metal bar that fitted into the steering wheel and, when locked, prevented it from turning. It was heavily advertised as the answer to rising car theft rates. There was even a small payment if you lost your car while using The Club. Even such measures may not be enough. When Danna parked in a bad part of town, outside the hospital to which she was posted, their car was stolen, The Club and all. A day or so later, it was found, stripped down and abandoned.

"How did they do it?" Danna asked the police. "I had The Club on the steering wheel."

"You don't understand, do you?" the police officer replied, world-weary. "These guys were pros. Club?

Steering wheel? Lady, that's long gone. The whole dashboard is gone."

Newspaper reports unveiled a newer way to steal a car. It did not happen when the owner was absent and the anti-theft device – whether the Club or ignition cut-off – was enabled. The method was used when the driver was in the car, the keys conveniently in the ignition. At stop signs and traffic lights, a person leapt out, pulled the victim driver out from the car and took over the wheel. In some cases – where the car was locked or there was a struggle – the driver might be summarily shot. In one case, the car theft cum shooting involved two Japanese students driving a new Honda. It took place in Anaheim, California; that is near Disneyland, the epitome of wholesome America.

Another example of escalating violence and lack of gun control among Americans: it would be too easy to jump to that conclusion. In this case, however, the car-jackers were Chinese. Their exploits, moreover, were aimed at exports. The booming economy in China had created great demands for luxury sedans and sportscars. Since these were subject to high taxes and red tape, a trans-Pacific black market had emerged. The car thieves smuggled the cars across the ocean to evade taxes. The Chinese buyers saved money and waiting time. The American insurance companies paid out to victims. Someone along the way fixed the bullet holes and shampooed the upholstery to remove any blood stains.

The violent commerce seemed wholly alien to me, unbelievable. Living in America, with newspapers so full of such violence, I quickly learnt to just shake my head and keep going. And between disbelief and indifference, it was easy to feel this when it was happening to someone else. All I had was a second-hand, non-luxury car. For me, there was no personal threat from such episodes. It just meant higher insurance rates – a big 20 per cent addition to the originally modest price tag of the car. In the end, the car I bought had an electronic ignition cut-off to prevent theft. But I did not invest in bullet-proof windows.

❖

There are certain negative stereotypes about Asians and cars in America. The first is that Asians drive badly. The second, more prevalent in California than other places, is that if you see a new Merc or sportscar, it is likely to have an Asian driving it. Whether envy links the two is debatable.

Living in America, Ken was aware of both stereotypes. He consciously defied them. He drove a slightly dented, ten-year-old Honda hatchback. As a researcher in a bio-technology lab, he could have afforded more, perhaps a Beemer. But he seemed proud of the fact that the old Honda was fully paid up and, with a roof rack, serviceable and useful. It went against the stereotype of Asians and flashy cars. He also drove it like a professional. He made a point of knowing the streets so he never got lost or wandered into the wrong lane. Ken drove so that he zipped into empty spaces, never giving other drivers an excuse to honk him. If Asians were known in America as bad drivers, Ken was not someone contributing to that bad rep.

"The drivers here suck," he said as we sped through the streets. He recalled the simpler ways in Oregon, where he used to live: "People there observed four-way stop signs. We gave way to each other. Out here, it's dog eat dog. It's a war zone." A black Dodge tried to cut into our lane. Ken honked him. The car honked back. Windows came down as the two cars sped along, next to each other.

"You asshole!" the driver of the Dodge, a White man, yelled.

"No, you're the asshole!" Ken shouted back, refusing to be intimidated, perhaps because another stereotype was that Asian men were milder than Americans. Ken made a fist and pointed his middle finger at the man. The all-American signal was reflected back.

"Not me! You're the asshole!"

"No! You, you are the asshole!"

"You asshole!"

"No, you're the asshole!"

The exchange continued with increasing anger and volume, but little variation. At the next junction, the Dodge turned left. We went straight on. Ken became quickly calm. "Drivers here suck," he reiterated flatly. I told him about cut-and-thrust traffic in Singapore. About incidents of car bullies and fights. About the unlikeliness of anyone voluntarily giving anyone else way. Things were worse in Bangkok, Manila, other Asian capitals. Ken shook his head in disbelief. He had forgotten such things.

"Things are bad here," he said. "But no one stops to do battle with a crow bar." Then another car tried to cut in on him. Ken slapped the horn, loud: "C'mon! For Chrissakes!"

Driving in the countryside was different. The late summer sun was warm. The hills and coastline, vast and grand. On a winding but well-paved coastal road, the city, its traffic and threat of crime, receded with the miles. Along the way, my car passed, or was passed by, huge jeeps, pick-ups and tank-like recreational vehicles – automobiles that typify the American's visits to the countryside. Jin and I had decided on a Honda Civic, a car small enough for the narrow streets of Cambridge but with an injected engine to give it some highway pep. But as we drove on, I thought of buying American, perhaps of getting a jeep. If a car was part of the American dream, then a bigger car constituted a large claim on that dream.

I refuelled at a petrol station. Or, to use the American term, "gas pump". The pump attendant began to complain about President Bill Clinton's move to raise a gas tax. It was only a few cents more per gallon. I watched the meter of the gas pump; the cents increased so slowly. I thought of telling the attendant that gas prices in America were still among the lowest in the world. Of telling him that, per person, Americans consume more of this energy source than any other people in the world, that the low price does not reflect the scarcity of oil or its full toll on the environment. But I had begun to see things from his view. The long distances that must be travelled; the lack of public transport; the right, dammit, to pursue the American way of life in a car. So I just added my tankful to the vast ocean of America's consumption and drove on into the distance.

The small town we arrived at seemed cosy. It sat on the coast. Two main streets with some shops and restaurants around a picturesque and sheltered harbour. We parked the car and, after a little tour, settled for an early night into a comfortable country inn, run by an old couple. I woke the next morning and went out to take in the country air. There was a man sitting on the porch of a light-blue clapboard house, resting after mowing the lawn, smoking a pipe. He was the neighbour and had been chatting with the owners of the inn. I took a short walk. Then, after a leisurely country-style breakfast of dollar pancakes, bacon and syrup, I asked if I could join them on the porch. Yes, of course, I could join them, they said. No, of course I was not intruding. Most Americans are friendly. A nod or smile is often enough to start a conversation, especially in smaller towns like this one. So I sat down to soak up some small town talk, part of the atmosphere of being in such a place.

"This town isn't safe anymore," the man surprised me by beginning. I looked around at the idyllic scene. How dangerous could it be here? I waited for the man's terrible example of crime. He continued, "We used to just leave the car doors unlocked and the keys in the ignition. These days you have to be careful. Just last year, someone had his car stolen." With a sigh, he added, "It's not like it used to be."

The others nodded and joined in, elaborating this tale of a single car theft. The discussion went on as if it were the crime of the century. They were well-meaning enough to advise me, a stranger, to be careful. "I'd lock my car if I was you." I nodded at their warnings, not wanting to tell them that I – city-trained – already had, of course. And armed my anti-theft device too.

The nightmares of theft, of crime and violence, might be crowding in elsewhere. But in this town, a single car theft, a whole year ago, was still worth talking about. It was still so safe. So it must be, I realised then, in many other places in this country beyond the big cities. I sat, and the conversation moved onto more pleasant things, a meandering gossip about local people and things to see and do in the area, the prospect of a warm summer and good fishing. It was a lazy, pleasant exchange befitting a country morning. I was glad to have come, to have driven this way.

You buy the car and into the American dream. Only then the full costs and dangers become visible. These could have been my conclusions from driving only in the city. But there was also the fresh, safe air of the countryside and small towns, and hundreds of miles to go. At the end of the morning, we went to the car. It was still sitting there, on the quiet street next to the clapboard house, in the small harbour town: my stake in the American dream. Not stolen, broken into or vandalised; steering column intact, theft-proof system still working. I thought about the dangers of the city and reluctantly drove back.

holidays,
disasters & american friends

DRIVING THROUGH a quiet neighbourhood on Halloween, there are reasons to be concerned, even scared. It is not that Halloween is frightening. Although distantly connected to ancient, more serious rituals such as All Souls' Day, it has become something that is celebrated by kids in costume, dressed as witches and other ghouls, going from door to door, yelling, "Trick or treat!" You have to give them a treat: sweets, chocolates or caramel apples. If not, you may suffer soap on your windows, an upturned flower pot or some other trick. America has somehow turned an originally dark event into a celebration of community, children, sweets and humour. Not dark and menacing, but cute: kitsch.

At least, that's the way it was. It might still be so in smaller towns and safer neighbourhoods. In such a context, the uniquely American tradition is harmless, even charming. But elsewhere, fear had returned in a newer context. Treats had turned into mistreatment: chocolates spiked with poison and apples with embedded razors. Children pretending to be monsters of the night had been accosted and abused by adults who were. While these incidents had been few and far between, it did not take much to instil fear at Halloween.

Yet this threat of physical harm to children was not the main controversy when I was in America. The issue was psychological harm and prejudice. This was started by a community school in the traditional Mid-West which issued guidelines decreeing what costumes children should avoid at Halloween. Witches were objectionable because they denigrated women. Black-face outfits offended African-Americans. Dressing like a hobo abused the homeless. This politically correct costume code had been jeered by some people and parents.

Between political correctness and physical dangers, the once innocent ceremony of Halloween had been complicated. Parents had now to decide what the kids should wear and whom it was safe to visit. Some limited visits to those neighbours they knew, thus narrowly delimiting their community and sense of neighbourliness. Most parents accompanied their children, chaperoning them from door to door. They taught them to say, "Thank you", and not to eat too many sweets. But their primary motive was protection.

Yet, it was not only the young that needed protection on Halloween night in America. I too was concerned. Not about bad-taste candy and costumes: the fear was caused by the tale of another Asian. Almost exactly a year before, he had been driving around, lost and late for a Halloween party – as I was that evening. The Asian, a college student, had then stopped at the wrong house. He went to the back to ask directions. The owner, a White American, came out with a gun, yelling, "Freeze!" The Asian continued to move forward, not understanding the colloquial American use of the word, smiling as the bullet was fired. His death and the killer's subsequent acquittal shocked some – especially in the Asian American community – as no fictional horror tale could.

When I arrived safely at the right address, I recounted the story of the Asian student to my hosts, Ann and Don Snodgrass. Ann frowned, and added her own tales of Halloween terror. "Some children take the tricks in trick or treat too far. Nowadays, windows get smashed, trash upturned in the street. It's vandalism. Still, I hope some children come out this Halloween," she said anxiously. "Last year, there were so few of them."

"There'll be more this year," her daughter, Jackie, assured us. As a grade-school teacher, Jackie had heard about the politically correct costume guidelines, "No, our school didn't follow that. Whatever they want to wear is fine by us, so long as they take part. That's what we really encourage. Halloween is a tradition, part of growing up. Some of them even brought their costume to class. They're so cute." Mother and daughter smiled and reminisced about the old days, tricks done, treats received and costumes once worn. The Snodgrasses had lived here for more than 20 years Jackie and her elder brother, now living in Chicago, grew up in this neighbourhood and went to school here. While Ann prepared our supper, Don and Jackie took us for a walk around the neighbourhood. The trees were almost bare and there was a wind blowing. It was cold; winter was in the air.

Jackie remained warm, talkative. She pointed out the houses that had paid particular attention to Halloween decorations. She told us about making Jack-o-Lanterns, carving the orange pumpkin that ripens during this season to make a scary head, lit by candles placed inside it. She showed us the school she went to, a red brick building just over a hill from the Snodgrass home. In their youth, during Halloween, Jackie and her brother had haunted these same streets. Grown up now, walking along with her father, but without costume, she talked about neighbours, people Jackie went to school with, old friends in this community. Halloween was a tradition Jackie had loved as a child, and she continued with another generation.

This was what the Snodgrass family had invited me to witness. Not simply a fun occasion of costume and sweets, but a celebration of American tradition and community. We completed our walk and went back into the warm house. As my hosts told their tales, we all relaxed, smiling and drinking warm cider in the cosy living room, in a prosperous, upper-middle-class neighbourhood.

Then, two children knocked on the door. One was dressed as a spider. The other, a giant bat. Ann, the hostess, held out a generous tray of sweets for them to pick from. She and the children stood in the open door, in the porch lit in the gathering darkness by the candle-light from the Jack-o-Lantern. The children's mother, their chaperon, stood in the background, looking on with a smile. It seemed like a scene from the past, fit to be painted by Norman Rockwell or photographed and put into a family album.

No one pointed out how all the sweets on the tray were kept in their original wrapping as proof they had not been tampered with. No one mentioned politically correct costume, the acts of vandalism or the death of an Asian. No one discussed the dwindling sense of community in the darkness that was gathering outside, across America. The simple occurrence of these two children and their innocent interaction with Ann kept those troubles in abeyance. Celebrations are not, after all, the right time to dwell on bad things. Some things are too scary even for Halloween.

❖

Holidays make you think of family and friends. Being away from them during the holiday season doubles your sense of isolation and estrangement. America can be a lonely place. Not just for foreigners, but also for the millions of Americans who move from their homes for schools and jobs. Or those who no longer have a family. The cherished mobility of Americans can leave only a thin sense of community and belonging.

We were saved from that by the Snodgrasses, whom we first visited that Halloween. Don Snodgrass worked as an economist in a development institution that was associated with Harvard. With his wife Ann, a former nurse, they had spent several years in Malaysia and, more recently, in Indonesia. On those tenuous links of university and geographical region, the Snodgrasses became our host family. They were in their late 60s. Their children were almost our age.

They invited us into their home in Lexington, a half-hour outside of Cambridge, a pleasant and comfortable house on a quiet street opposite a church. They had us over on holidays, like Halloween and Thanksgiving, when their son and daughter-in-law came from Chicago for a family get-together. And they invited us out to their holiday home on Cape Cod, the thin arm of scenic land just outside Boston that reaches out into the Atlantic Ocean.

Ann became like an aunt to us. She helped us learn where we might find this or that item we were looking for. She lent us guide books on the New England region and even suggested where we might go for our wedding anniversary dinner. Once in a while, she called just to find out how we were. Don, a history buff, took us on a historical tour of the Lexington area, where the American revolution began with the first confrontations with the British Army. He talked to me about my thesis and sent me clippings of articles he had found useful. We chatted about Southeast Asian politics and economies, which he knew well. They were kinder than we, complete strangers, had any right to hope for. There was almost nothing, moreover, they wanted in return. The Snodgrasses only apologised when work or other duties prevented them from calling us more often. Whenever someone talks about American hospitality, I will think about Don and Ann.

I will also think about our neighbour, Helen. Not that she was as generous or congenial as Don and Ann – quite the contrary. When we first moved in, we asked her over for tea. The conversation was polite but awkward. Helen was not sociable. She seemed content to be on her own, to potter around the house and garden. She used to jog and do the marathon but developed chronic fatigue syndrome and had to stop. She went out at nights to learn country-style contra-dancing. She went alone but there were single men, elderly, and with no intent but a good old-fashioned dance. Helen did not complain outright but she seldom smiled. Few things made her happy.

Helen, like so many Americans we met, was divorced. Her son, in his 20s, had gone to university in another state, returning only for the occasional long weekend. Her father, in his 70s, had left her mother and lived in Maine, some three hours' drive to the north. He visited once in a while. We met briefly in the street, outside the house. He was a fairly tall man with a slight spread around his middle, a little bent with age but still looking healthy. However, the relationship between Helen and her father was strained. Helen told us candidly; she blamed him for breaking up with her mother and he chided her for splitting from her husband. They had not much to say to each other. She made sure that whenever he came to town, they would have tickets to the ball game so they could be together without having to say too much about anything that mattered. Still, unless someone – son or father – came to visit her, Helen was alone.

For that first Christmas in America, we went to Ken and Danna's house for dinner. We told them about

Helen. "Oh, that's typical," Danna said. Many Americans are alone. During the holidays, depression goes up. So does suicide, especially among those who live alone. As a doctor, Danna told us that the hospital psychiatric wards gear up for a busy time over the holiday season. So do radio talk shows, suicide help lines and shelters for the homeless. Families and friends move all across America and when holidays come, even the overcrowded airlines, trains and buses cannot bring everyone back together again.

Danna's own circumstances were not so different from Helen's. She was from Oregon, on the other side of the continent. Her parents had split up and she saw them once a year, separately. Living in Boston, she was cut off from the people she grew up with, went to school and university with. When she first arrived, she knew no one else besides Ken. He was no better, thousands of miles from his family in Singapore and the cities he had lived in before. He had just two house-mates he did not know well. The only difference between them and Helen, Danna pointed out, was that she and Ken had each other. Loneliness was therefore kept at bay. Their life together was not lonely but it was quiet. The Christmas dinner in their house, with us and a number of colleagues from work, was an exception of noise and celebration.

It was their first party in their new house, a lovely apartment in an old Victorian house, with finely-carved wood panelling and a fireplace. The table was laden with a 20-pound turkey and traditional trimmings – mashed potatoes, carrots and peas, cranberry sauce. Outside, the first snow had already fallen. This might very well have been the White Christmas that Bing Crosby promised but equatorial Singapore had never experienced. Inside, those who had fireplaces started their first fires for the cold season. It was a comfortable, sleepy, stay-in time of year for family – or, in this case, friends – and feasting.

The year ends early in America. After Thanksgiving, through Christmas and the Jewish Hanukah, and into the New Year, America enters an extended holiday. "Offices are on skeleton staff," explained Ken. "A lot of people are on leave. Things still get done but they do take it a little easier. Americans know when to work and when it's time to take a break." Danna saw things somewhat differently. "Just try getting anything done," she told us, "besides shopping, I mean."

I nodded, trying to stay awake after a full helping of holiday turkey. Danna was right: shopping was the exception. The one thing Americans do at year-end. Shops, unlike offices, are not on skeleton staff. They extend operating hours, hire extra part-timers, keep lights blazing and Christmas jingles jangling. That year, a shop owner told me, thanks to the slight but perceptible economic recovery, the crowds were back. It seemed as hectic as anything on Orchard Road.

In the well-known carol, Christmas has 12 gift-giving days. Americans, however, have gone far beyond that. The holiday starts in November, allowing a full month of shopping, with massive sales and discounts. From Thanksgiving onwards, stores compete madly for business, advertising discounts of 30, 50 per cent or more. Or two-for-one offers. Or special gift sets. Everything, from books to perfumes, from power tools to that massage shower you have always wanted is on offer. If America is the consummate consumer society, this is the time to watch them shop. America loves Christmas and its bargains. It is just the lack of parking space everyone hates.

Along New York's Fifth Avenue, I found block-long queues of shoppers outside the famous window-displays at Saks department store. At the Potomac Mills in Virginia, which touts itself as one of the world's largest shopping malls, the carpark was full, so were many of its shops.

With the economic recovery, most had predicted record sales. The actual results were good, but not as high as hoped. Many retailers – especially clothing stores – ended up overstocked. End-of-season sales kicked in to give an extra 25 to 50 per cent off. Credit terms were also made easy on cars and electrical appliances to clear. By such means, the American retailer entices those whose spirit is willing to spend but find their cash low. To see this in operation goes some way to understanding why America has become a country that lives on credit.

But consumer temptation is not the greatest danger in America. The ghost of Christmas present in America can be malevolent. Tired of crowds, I considered an easier way to shop, picking something from the pile of catalogues in the mailbox. Clothes, lingerie, pots and pans were lovingly photographed to entice you. Just flip the page, fill in the order form, enclose your cheque and send it off. You can even order by phone with your credit card number. In a week or so the parcel arrives. If it happens to be damaged or you simply change your mind, return it and get your money back. It was that easy. Or was it?

A small item in the newspaper and a brief mention on the local TV station set off alarms that rang louder than Christmas bells. Reports warned that fraud went up at this time of year. The crooks sent catalogues or called customers, offering unbelievable bargains. But if you gave in and used your credit card number, there was a chance that the company would re-use it fraudulently. With your credit card number, they would buy a thousand and one things at your expense. Instead of the goods you ordered, you got evil.

Theft, another news item warned, was also a seasonal activity. A pamphlet put out by a policemen's union in Boston, warned people about "Fear City USA". That was a sentiment that a tourist promotion council was unlikely to support, but it bordered on the truth. In the city's busiest shopping and tourist areas, there had been a spate of knife-point robberies and fights. *Don't stay out after 2 am; don't put your shopping bags in the car until you're ready to leave; tell the police if you're leaving your home for more than a few days* – this was some of the friendly advice the newspaper offered during the holiday season.

It is not that such crimes are unknown at other times of year. Rather, the difference is in where crime occurs. Come Christmas, the criminal elements that stay on the fringes of the city for the rest of year stray into the centre. In a society marked between the haves and have-nots, the tensions rise with shopping and feasting. The difference between the myth of a merry Christmas season and its realities is stark.

Yet, there are still safe and non-material aspects to the year's end in America. New York's swank Fifth Avenue is lit up. Holiday-makers skate on the ice-rink at the Rockefeller Centre and passers-by gawk at the grand Christmas tree. Even the notoriously discourteous native New Yorker seems to smile. In cities, homeless shelters report an upsurge in gifts of food and blankets, and volunteer helpers. Charities organise the collection of presents for poor children. On the political scene that year, First Lady Hillary Clinton helped set the mood. Over the season, she left aside her failing initiative at health care reform to volunteer her time to work in a soup kitchen for the homeless, and light the White House Christmas tree.

Back at the stores, there were many smiles. With the crowds and extra hours, those who served the endless rows of customers might have been frazzled and lacklustre. But, even without a Singapore-style courtesy campaign, those working in the stores and service sector largely continued to be helpful and patient. In one shop, they apologised that they had run out of the toys I wanted for my nephews. In another, when they did not have exactly what I was looking for, the sales assistant helpfully suggested another place to try, giving precise directions through the large mall. It was enough to remind me that America was first settled into not by traders but by religious puritans. Although they are now the world's prime consumer culture, some part of their spirit does not surrender to materialism. Some part of Americans still affirms a spirit of giving, especially at this time of year.

At Ken and Danna's house, after a hearty dinner, sitting beside the fire, we could feel that spirit and that warmth. It was warmth, both physical and emotional, that was needed at a time of cold weather and short days; at a time when America took a holiday from work but not from anxieties and problems; at a time for many in America, when it was a wary Christmas, rather than a merry one.

In many places and for many people, the season would bring happiness and special acts of kindness. Not everyone got robbed or ripped off. Many did not quarrel at their annual family gathering. Volunteers helped at homeless shelters. People donated turkeys and food to the poor. Friends, away from their families, got together. Strangers smiled more readily. Many would find themselves full and contented. In the American pursuit of happiness, for better or worse, Christmas holidays have a special significance. In this, we too had a place.

❖

The first time I saw snow in North America, it was from a cabin facing a lake. The picture-book scene made me think of Christmas store-fronts on Orchard Road with their styrofoam beads, and those water-filled globes children play with, turning them upside-down to bring a shower of snow flakes down on the miniature figures within. From such a vantage point, snow was idyllic, welcome. It was, however, very different when I was shovelling in the cold in the early morning to clear the porch and walkway, and the car was stuck deep in a two-foot high drift.

The New Year started with Northeasters – pronounced "Nor' Easters". Storms stretched from Washington DC to Maine, covering the East Coast with snow, cold winds and, worse, an icy coating of sleet and freezing rain. As if to christen my time in the country, the winter brought a historic high snowfall, exceeding all records for the last 100 or so years.

At three in the morning, a whir of sounds brought me to the window to see an object moving through the darkness, lit up by flashing yellow lights like a UFO. It was a pick-up truck with a tractor-like shovel secured to its front bumper. Municipal authorities had sent out work crews and snow ploughs to clear the roads. By morning, there was more than a metre of snow. Traffic was down to a crawl. Airports across the country experienced long delays and closures. In West Virginia, power lines were down, leaving 200,000 people without electricity. In Cambridge, two men past 70 years of age died that day, while engaged in the seemingly simple act of shovelling their sidewalks.

Another storm came, depositing a further half metre or more of snow. I had to go out again, shovel in hand. "It's not too bad so far," my neighbour, John Hopkins, chatted as we both shovelled. "You should have seen the blizzard we had in March last year. Now, that was bad. Much worse." To keep warm, I pulled my hood low over my face; he could not see my look of incredulity. How could things be worse? But John was right: America was used to worse.

Through that week and despite subsequent storms, cities were able to keep their essential services going. Each house, including ours, had stocked up on a snow shovel, an ice-scraper and a spray to free locks on doors and cars when they had frozen up. Most people lived up to their civic duty to keep the sidewalk outside their house clear of snow. Constant weather and news updates kept everyone forewarned, and prepared for more storms. Life went on, more or less normally.

We went out on foot because parking in many areas was prohibited during the snow emergency. Tramping through thick piles of snow, treading gingerly around rivers of slushy, brown melt on the roads, I was reminded of the floods Singapore used to have: the sense of living through emergencies. The underground train stations were mucky and more crowded than usual. But still, the trains ran. Our way was slowed by the ice-slicked pavements and the pools of dirty melt-water we had to skirt around. The traffic was snarled. But there was electricity in the cinema and more than comfortable heating. So in the middle of a record snowstorm, we watched a movie set in sunny Mexico.

On the way home, we dropped off a package. Our fax modem needed repair and was to be sent right across the continent to the manufacturers. "No problem," the courier company said, despite the circumstances. "It'll be there tomorrow." At the supermarket, there were longer lines but no danger that food supplies would run low. New York alone spent more than $10 million on facing that first snow storm. Many other cities would also dig deep into their budgets. But compared to the floods in the Mid-West, hurricanes in the south and earthquakes in California, this was a seasonal inconvenience, not a national crisis. America had the wherewithal to meet this emergency, in ways that smaller and poorer countries could not.

When we bumped into our neighbour Hilary Hopkins, she told us about her nightmare week. To escape the snow and cold that had engulfed the East Coast, she had flown to California. She was then caught in an LA earthquake. Her 15th-floor hotel room swayed but held and now she was glad to be back in her stable, warm house. "It was terrible," she said with an incongruously bright smile, dusting the snow from her down jacket. "I'm so glad to back, despite the snow. I can always stay indoors."

Hilary's story illustrated how most people experienced the natural calamities of earthquake and snowstorms that winter: fleetingly, cushioned from impact, able to retreat from it by plane or by going into a well-heated house. America and most Americans have the resources to meet such emergencies. However, there were exceptions. In LA, most of the media had emphasised that the quake brought the city together, overcoming racial problems. But while many had suffered, the impact had been greatest among the poor. One of the first victims was a Latino immigrant, sweeping up a carpark in the pre-dawn hours when a building fell. Why, one Hispanic commentator asked in the New York Times, was he there?

Richer, mainly White suburbanites rushed to city emergency shelters. They banked on insurance and savings to rebuild. By contrast, many poorer city-dwellers were camped in parks, fashioning tents from blankets – among tens of thousands the quake had made homeless. As state and federal authorities brought help, the question became who would get it first. An angry crowd of about 4,000 crammed into a single disaster-relief centre demanding attention.

The East Coast snowstorms were a quieter emergency but the contrast between rich and poor was also mirrored in the frozen pavements. Along New York's fancy Madison Avenue, the homeless huddled in cardboard boxes and blankets. They spent the cold night in front of stylish art galleries and designer stores like the Versace boutique, hoping not to freeze to death.

City shelters allowed over 6,000 people to come inside for the night but many refused, despite record low temperatures. "Some guys get robbed," one explained, "some guys get stabbed." Crowded shelters and a shortage of beds were other reasons put forward. The poor who had a roof over their heads were off the streets, less visible. Yet among these, there were many who could not afford heating – which could easily come to $100 to $200 per month – and still risked their health.

Neither the winter storm nor earthquake brought much public comment on the problems of the poor and what to do in the longer term. Some in LA noted the string of catastrophes the city had faced, starting from the riots of 1992. There was, however, no correlation to the attempts after those riots to bring longer-term help and jobs. Those efforts, that started with so much publicity and optimism, had become mired in frustration and marked by resignations of top officials in the effort to re-build LA, including its original head. The earthquake did not, in the long term, change the landscape. The winter storms did not bring the poor in from the cold.

Underlying natural disasters, there were man-made problems. The poor, unlike fallen highways or frozen-in cities, did not feature in television clips, but they too were revealed in the present misfortunes. When the aftershocks were over, however, when temperatures rose and public attention had moved to something else, the problems of the poor remained. In his classic book, *Democracy in America*, De Tocqueville wrote, "Nothing struck me more forcibly than the general equality of condition among the people." One hundred and fifty years later, an earthquake and record cold temperatures brought notice of a change to that situation.

When I ran an errand in Harvard Square during the bad weather, I kept a look-out for Harvie, from whom I always bought my copy of *Spare Change*. He was not there. There was no one begging at the street corners. The pavements, the whole Square, were icy. The snow turned grey-brown. People were tired – from driving, walking and weathering the storm. They went from store to store, one warm place to another, their heads bowed, as quickly as the bad conditions allowed. They were surly in queues, honked loudly in traffic jams. My hope was that Harvie and the other homeless had found a shelter until warmer weather and moods returned to the Square.

After yet another snowfall and shovelling session, we had had enough. We went out of the city. In the countryside too, it was cold and the snow covered the ground. But it was a thick white blanket rather than brown slush; there were hill slopes in place of icy pavements. Important differences. If it was going to snow this much, we might as well be skiing. This was only our second time. Without lessons, we spent almost as much time falling as skiing. We did not mind. If I was going to ache, it might as well be from skiing, rather than shovelling. Others had the same idea. The ski resort was full.

After two slow seasons, a ski instructor said things were picking up. All the ski lifts were working. Machines churned out man-made snow to add to the slopes. The instructor, a tall, big-boned blonde, flitted between different ski resorts across the continent. Mostly, out west at Jackson Hole in Wyoming and other star resorts; now, on the eastern seaboard with its smaller peaks and sometimes icy-snow. Without another steadier job, she – like so many in this industry – was dependent on snow and a good, high-income winter season. For her, and the resort, the snowstorms that inconvenienced everyone else were good news.

Charges for a day of skiing were about $50 to $70, including ski rental. Lessons went for between $30 to $50 per hour. Skiing is a sport for the better-off American, not Harvie and others who have no choice but to be out in the snow. The Kohs enrolled their children in a ski school. Soon, Jonathan and Michael were among the throngs of smaller kids, fearlessly and seemingly effortlessly hurtling themselves downhill. Another Singaporean,

Jacky, went out almost every weekend. Before long, he was trying out the hardest black diamond trails. After a bad first experience, Jin Hua too was hooked. The combination of exhilarating speed and beautiful scenery of the white slopes: skiing was that sort of experience. Despite slips and bad starts, a newcomer in America had to get up and go again. Back outside, I fell down once more and just lay there for a while, my back inch-deep in the white powder. I looked up and against the sky, and saw the snow from the snow-making machines shooting upwards and then cascading down. The city and its ice-induced problems seemed far away. From some vantage points, I realised, more snow was always welcome.

tv images

"MEN AREN'T interested in what's on TV," the female stand-up comic quipped, mimicking someone holding a remote control. "They're interested in what *else* is on." At first, I didn't quite get it, like many other American jokes. It was not me losing my sense of humour or the way she told the joke. If you don't know, for example, who Rush Limbaugh is, or the latest Hollywood gossip, some jokes are going to pass you by in the USA. Especially with stand-up comedy, that especially American phenomenon. Even if you speak English, you need news, names and a mass of trivia as a cultural background to understanding.

Accustomed to a choice of just six channels on Singaporean and Malaysian TV, I didn't get the joke about men and the remote control. Then we installed cable service. The installation took mere minutes and two short cables. The cost was less than a dollar a day. For that came over 60 channels. I could have gotten more: 80 to 120 stations is quite common. Or else, I could have had my own satellite dish. That was down to about 18 inches across and less than $1,000: smaller and cheaper than ever before. But 60-some channels was enough for me, at least for a start. Enough to introduce me to American culture.

The Kohs did not have cable. "It's because of the kids," Linus told us. "There's too much violence on TV. You should see the cartoons, let alone the real-life cop shows and the news. We let them watch TV only on Saturday mornings. Even that's probably too much. But they're already starting to ask for more. When they go to school the other kids talk about shows they haven't seen."

"Oh, Dad!" Jonathan, their eldest, chimed in. "It's not so bad."

"It's just TV," Michael, the middle child, argued precociously. It was obviously a long-running protest against a decision that the children accepted but wished were otherwise.

The boys had a marked American accent, TV or not. "Yeah," Karen admitted. "Don't you just hate it? I try to correct them, but there's nothing I can do. It's the way everyone in school speaks. And they want to fit in, so they speak that way too."

"It's also what they hear on TV," Linus concluded, having quelled the boys' protests again, this time at least. "Do you have any idea how much time most American kids spend in front of the TV? Way too much time."

At primetime, I began my exploration of the airwaves. I started with warlords in Somalia, moved to

Seinfeld, then – in quick succession – MTV's top hits, a made-for-TV thriller, a Congress discussion of NAFTA, wrestling, an "I Love Lucy" re-run, local weather and a 1990 blockbuster movie. Then it was "David Letterman's Late Show", at midnight. I pressed on, with both time and the remote control.

I went further through the electronic medium, discovering more obscure paths. On another channel, there was a discussion forum on serious political subjects, the market place of ideas. The speakers interrupted each other to grab that spotlight of electronic attention. They spat out policies and philosophy in sound-bites of ten seconds or less. There were shopping channels that plied late-night viewers with all types of products, endorsed by former TV stars like Morgan Brittany and Connie Stevens – names and faces you vaguely remember for products you vaguely need. Every day, for 24 hours, through a toll-free number and credit card, through the TV supermarket you can buy, buy and buy.

In some five hours, I had run the gamut from serious to funny, real action to Hollywood acting, politics to shopping. I had travelled around the world and back, seeing both trouble spots a continent away and sunny spots for the local weather in the next three days. The media was like a magic carpet or better. All this was done, without even leaving the room or even – thanks to the remote control – my seat. As Max Lerner observed in the classic *America as a Civilisation*, television brings "the world to the home, wrapped up in a single gleaming febrile package".

Television is the definitive American medium. It was first invented, promoted and made commercial in this country. It provides a mass culture, a set of reference points to which every American relates – from small town to big city, from one corner of this vast country to the opposite end, to rich and poor alike. It is taught in schools; not just to those who want to make TV shows, run the cameras and lights but also to those who might want to, say, make a study of "Bewitched" or the "Brady Bunch" as commentaries on the family roles of their times.

The cable revolution is changing television. It is no longer a mass media in the sense that people are treated as a mass amalgam with only a few choices. Rather, because there are now so many choices, it is rapidly becoming a world of differentiated media. With the multiplication of channels, there is a splintering of markets: MTV and a number of rival channels provide an endless stream of music videos; another pumps out "I Love Lucy" and other 1960s re-runs, or news; a third provides 24-hour comedy shows. Instead of "broadcasting", people have begun to talk about "narrow-casting", to describe this more targeted approach.

Still, there can be 120 channels and nothing on that's worth watching. The problem is that you can't believe that, and so flick on from one channel to the next, hopeful, attentive for the few seconds it takes to decide to move on. By the time all channels are exhausted, nearly an hour has passed. So you think that, now, there must be something new that's worth watching. And you begin again. That was my experience. When, finally, I switched the whole thing off, the silence in my home was deafening. The stillness, dizzying. Then I fell into a numb sleep.

The next morning, talking to some Americans, the conversation was about the abrupt cancellation of Chevy Chase's talk show – which they thought tedious. Then the Letterman top ten list of reasons why Hillary was smarter than Bill (Americans love being on a first-name basis with their first couple) – which they found Hillaryous.

Educated by the TV, a bulb had clicked on somewhere in the thought balloon above my head. I understood the conversation and the jokes. I could join in and comment on the common discourse that mass media creates to bind this continent together. A survey has shown that, on average, Americans watch TV for more than five hours a day. As much as I did on that first night; perhaps too much. It detracted, I found, from time for work, reading and other forms of leisure. I also realised that much of what I learnt grew quickly out of date and irrelevant. David Letterman tells different jokes each night and the White House continually holds press conferences and events. News must be new, after all. The mass American culture is a wasting asset, notwithstanding re-runs, that requires a continual investment of time. The work involved, moreover, may not be worth it. Much of it was, after all, just a joke.

I felt tired. The overload of information bred an inertia, a passivity. Satiated on TV, entertainment and the visual, I felt little need to know more; to seek a deeper understanding of the issues behind the images. Rather, it was a compulsion to flick on another channel. A commentator on American culture, Neil Postman, warned that Americans were "entertaining themselves to death". By this, he meant more than just increasing the number of hours spent on cable and other forms of entertainment. He also meant an attitude that seeks to make everything entertaining or, otherwise, to ignore it. The news programmes are a prime example of this. American news on the main channels has increasingly become less analytical. Serious subjects are given short shrift. Instead, short, punchy and colourful presentations of quasi-news — celebrities, oddities, scandals and press conferences — prevail. The news stations claim they are necessary. Without them, they will lose the viewer's vagrant attention to a glitzier, shallower channel. I understood that after I got cable. Just as I could understand the jokes in late-night comedy. Not least, the one about men and remote control buttons. What else is on?

❖

In November each year, Americans pause to remember the day, more than thirty years ago now, when John F. Kennedy was killed. With that bullet, the young American president became an enduring American legend no one seems to want to forget. After him, innocence and optimism gave way to the killings of Martin Luther King and Bobby Kennedy, to Vietnam and Watergate. Everyone remembers, it has often been observed, where they were when they heard of Kennedy's death. And, perhaps even more, everyone knows where they, and America, have gone since.

A yearning for what might have been leads many to put aside Kennedy's actual record. He is not primarily remembered for his handling of the Cuban missile crisis or civil rights initiatives. Nor are his personal indiscretions – which would sink almost any living politician – held against him. Nostalgia puts the focus on his potential and image. A poll on recent presidents gave Kennedy the highest approval rating at 78 per cent, almost a third more than the next best. Beyond America, his portrait is said to have been seen in African and Asian villages to which he once sent Peace Corps volunteers. At home, books analysing his election victory and 1,000 days in office were on my father's shelf, to be among the first histories I read about America. So the man became myth; John Fitzgerald Kennedy became JFK.

Each November brings a surge of Kennedy memorials. It is not, however, a quiet time of national mourning. It is showbiz. Many in the public eye are anxious to associate themselves with that myth. The Kennedy clan has a natural claim. Headed by Senator Ted Kennedy, they are still active in politics and the lustre of the Kennedy name is founded on JFK's legend. The clan makes an annual pilgrimage to Arlington, where the widow Jackie is also now buried, in the full glare of television cameras. President Clinton was not too shy to tell the tale of how he, then a teenager, thrust himself forward to shake JFK's hand. Clinton came to Boston especially for the re-opening of the JFK library, a monumental glass-and-chrome structure on a narrow headland with spectacular views of the bay and the city. He did not discourage those who compliment him and his wife as being the most charismatic first couple since Jack and Jackie. One of his cabinet, Attorney-General Janet Reno, drew explicit parallels at a talk I attended. The task of the Clinton administration, she said, is to "engage in the great work of rebuilding this country". The words she used are those of Bobby Kennedy when he served in his brother's cabinet, also as attorney-general. Reno was speaking at a ceremony in memory of Bobby Kennedy after being introduced by his daughter, Kerry.

Politicians are not the only people to use the JFK myth. Books on JFK and the Kennedy clan could fill a wall of shelves. *JFK*, the movie by Oliver Stone, raked in millions with speculations of a conspiracy, refuting the official version that the killer, Oswald, acted alone. On TV, documentaries and docudramas abound, especially during November. Their timing is partly to mark the assassination – appropriate, for the telegenic Kennedy was, after all, the first television president.

Equally and less appropriately, there is another reason. According to media consultants, the JFK-linked shows are used by TV stations to bolster viewer ratings during the time when advertisers are assessing the different channels. The focus of the coverage was disturbing. Most shows contentedly wove familiar clippings of the photogenic president. Two shows dramatised JFK's youth, romances and all. Several morbidly focused on the assassination and its aftermath; one was a six-hour replay of the original TV footage while another dedicated itself wholly to Oswald the killer. Another let people recall their reactions to the killing. Everyone from former president Gerald Ford and journalist Walter

Cronkite to actor Michael Douglas and phone-in callers had a story to tell about where they were when they heard. Even the Thanksgiving special of TV's favourite country folk, the Waltons, centred on JFK's death. From almost a dozen programmes, only one sought to actually assess Kennedy's record as a president and politician. Questions about his death were featured much more than what JFK had lived for.

"College students today," a history professor commented, "consider Kennedy a figure from the Dark Ages." Students were quoted as saying JFK is "greater dead than alive". As such, JFK seems in danger of being treated on the same level as James Dean or Elvis. A celebrity, an item of trivia, a face and name to be endorsed on souvenirs, to be sighted in Las Vegas, with or without UFOs. The Kennedys who are alive contribute to that status. Several regularly make the pages of the American tabloids: John junior, JFK's son, once cavorted with movie star Darryl Hannah; Congressman Joseph Kennedy, Robert's son, had his marriage annulled and then remarried; Maria Shriver Kennedy is a TV celebrity and Arnold Schwarzenegger's wife. Teddy, the last brother, is still worth headlines even if he has sobered up. The Kennedys are America's royal family.

I was therefore curious enough to meet one of them. Kerry Kennedy came to the law school to give a talk about the work of a centre established in her father's name, the Robert F. Kennedy Center for Human Rights. The seminar room was emptier than I had expected, with perhaps some 30 people in the audience. Kerry Kennedy is one of the lesser celebrities in the clan, being neither a politician nor the subject of tabloid scandals. She does, however, undertake worthy work and gave a credible but not inspiring speech. Later, when I was introduced briefly, she talked about human rights in Ireland. Her sister had married one of the accused in the famous case that was then made into the movie *In the Name of the Father*, starring Daniel Day Lewis. That Hollywood connection remained.

I asked her whether she felt that being a Kennedy had helped her in het work. She seemed a little offended at first. Then she allowed that the centre did have more influence because of its connection to her father and that she, as its director, was able to use that influence for the good. She reeled off names of prisoners of conscience that she and the RFK Center had been able to help. What was important, she said, momentarily clenching her fist and tensing her small frame, was that the Kennedy name be used for the good. She too came in the name of the father.

❖

One Friday evening, a single star took over TV: every single channel. There was no other news. Normal programs were shelved, pre-empted. Even the all-important finals of the National Basketball Association championships were reduced to a small insert on the screen. The World Cup soccer games faded into even greater obscurity. The dominant image on every major channel was a white Ford Bronco driving along a highway. It was OJ Simpson, running ahead of a phalanx of police cars along a normally jammed highway. Ten or more helicopters belonging to TV stations hovered, broadcasting the scene live. At times, the cameras of one station blocked another's helicopter. The commentary from each was almost identical, dishing out banal and scanty information. Yet, no one could stop talking about OJ Simpson and his arrest for the bloody murder of his former wife and her male friend.

But, more than a story of mayhem, it was equally a tale about the American media. Since his arrest, speculation flooded TV, tabloids and newspapers on every detail, from OJ's mental state to the disputed forensic evidence and the possible death penalty. Everyone who played golf with OJ was hired to counter-check police evidence. Anybody who claimed to have seen him around the time of the killing was interviewed by the media. Prosecutors, defence attorneys, OJ's friends and countless others all held news conferences, playing the media game.

Everyone was talking about it, the hottest item on the agenda that the media set. There was little else to watch or read about. More than 95 million Americans watched Simpson and the police cars drive down the highway. There were almost 750 press stories within a week of the case – three to eight times more than earlier big news items like Tonya Harding arranging for rival Olympic skater Nancy Kerrigan to be beaten up, and the accusations that Michael Jackson molested a boy.

"There's no way he can be guilty," a man in his 50s told me in a supermarket queue. "I've seen him play football. You can't play like that and be someone who can kill his wife."

"It's a conspiracy," a young African-American said at the bicycle shop. "The White establishment wants to destroy any strong man of colour."

"This is a feminist issue," a woman at the university said. "He should never have been let off so easily for beating his wife in the first place. And now, there is symbolic justice that the prosecuting attorney is a woman. If only she didn't dress so badly."

"I can tell you what I think, but I can't say too much," a student at the law school confided. "I might be selected to help the defence counsel. Alan Dershowitz is on the Simpson defence team, you know."

Everyone was talking about OJ. To some, the story was about the fall of an American hero: OJ was in the Hall of Fame, was a TV sports commentator and starred in movies; he endorsed products like Hertz rental cars; he seemed like a nice guy. To others, it was about domestic violence and wife-beating, especially since Simpson had been caught on a previous occasion. Whatever it was, the superstar suspect overshadowed contemporaneous problems in Rwanda or the doubtful health of Clinton's health policy initiative. Like cars that usually jam the highway, such lesser news items had been cleared to make way for OJ and his white Ford Bronco. No detail was too small or petty. No observation too banal to be left unsaid. The pre-trial hearings were aired live and dragged on for hours – a startling occurrence in a world that seemingly lives on the three-second sound-bite.

"I don't want to talk about it," an American friend confessed at a garden party, a gathering of academics, activists and graduate students on the lawn of a professor from the law school. "There must be something else to talk about."

"It's just too trashy," another American continued. "Tabloid junk."

"What I can't stand," the first resumed, "is the media. How can they take it seriously? Why is it more important than Bosnia or a new gun law?"

From the OJ Simpson case, we debated about other matters. Those gathered turned to discussing the media's coverage, going over every detail with the finer, glossier focus of a serious subject: the media.

Publicity might have been one reason for OJ's ride in the white Bronco. In his would-be suicide note, Simpson hoped that the media would spare his young children from too much attention and let them lead normal lives. Media also threatened OJ's trial. After this news saturation, there was every danger that, although he had pleaded not guilty, a fair trial would be impossible. This case might well be decided by the press and public sympathy, and not a courtroom jury.

If OJ the nice guy was guilty, the distance between that image and the real man would be revealed, as would a more general truth about the media itself. This truth is that the American media is not wholly investigative and relentless for truth as some claim, that it can deceive and conceal as often as it reveals. The OJ case seems to speak of more than a twin murder by a former football star. If OJ was guilty, he showed that someone could stand in the limelight and the American media would not learn the truth about him or her until there was blood and a car chase.

❖

Peter Nazareth is now a famous American. A Goan originally from Uganda, he had come to the USA after the dictator Idi Amin expelled all Asians in the 1970s. Peter, as an academic and writer, found refuge at the University of Iowa as part of the well-known international writing programme. But his fame in the USA did not come from those accomplishments. It came from the fact that he taught a university course on Elvis. Because of that, Peter had been on most of the prime morning and evening news shows, like "Nightline", with Ted Koppel, and "Good Morning America". Tabloid TV shows, the USA Today newspaper and magazines followed up. Then Peter and his wife were guests of honour in Memphis, given the keys to the city and a VIP tour of Elvis's mansion, Graceland.

When Peter was in Boston to visit his daughter, he called and we met in Harvard Square. He wore brown pants and a beige shirt, with a native American locket and belt buckle. He talked quickly, affably and with unwavering enthusiasm. His head of curly, dark hair bobbed up and down as he spoke. About Third World literature, writing in Singapore, the African-American novelist Ishmael Reed. About mutual friends and old stories of the time we spent in Iowa together. Despite his new-found fame, Peter remained the same. Over Thai food, he filled me in on what had happened with his teaching of "Elvis as Anthology".

According to Peter, Jin Hua and I were there at the beginning. In 1990, when we met him in Iowa, he was just starting to assemble the course. I remembered an evening spent listening to music. Peter enthusiastically pulling out old LPs to compare, one after another, a song played by one Black musician or another, followed by the cover version done by The King. "It was not that Elvis imitated them or stole their music," Peter explained. "He synthesised it, and made it better. Look at the movie *Kid Creole*. A 'creole' is a mixture, something that is a bit of everything." The Elvis that Peter Nazareth saw was part Native American, part poor White Southerner, influenced by Black music, blues and gospel: hybrid.

Similarly, Peter never agreed with those who felt that that Elvis sold out in going to the army and then into slick, light-weight movies. He looked at Elvis's movies and found strong social content instead. "He was dangerous to the White establishment. Rock-n-roll was dangerous. Look at what happened to all the others. Elvis had to trick them. He wasn't a bad actor. That was his way of showing the audience that the role didn't interest him. That it wasn't really him. When there was a chance, he sneaked in something that was important. Look at the movie *Stay Away Joe*. Elvis is playing a half-Indian. In the end, the whole house — built from modern, White methods — comes down. What does that mean?" In Peter's analysis, even Elvis's Las Vegas jump suits with their fringe tassels and quasi-Aztec designs were significant.

But while interesting, the Elvis course did not become nationally known simply because of Peter's views or teaching. "It really had something to do with Singapore, actually," Peter explained. "After you left Iowa, I put the things together for the course and started teaching. People signed up, of course, but there was no big bang. Then Pat – remember Pat from Singapore, who came to Iowa to do a Master's? – well, she needed to do a story for an assignment in her mass communications and media course. So she asked if she could interview me. She came over and I played the records, just like I played them for you and Jin. Then, when she completed the article, it was published in the local Iowa City newspaper.

"A Cedar Rapids newspaper picked it up. Then it was in the national press. TV called up soon after. Ever since, radio shows and conferences have been calling me up for interviews and talks. I even get letters from people I've never met. People just interested in Elvis, and who want to talk about him. There is so much attention, because it's Elvis." And because of the media, I suggested.

"Yes, that's true. There's news about him every day, even if he's been dead for years. There's a whole book of stories about Elvis after death. The media love writing about Elvis and people love reading about him." Peter paused, rearranging the gold-rimmed spectacles on his nose. "And to think that Singaporeans were involved in getting the Elvis course known to America."

We both laughed and finished our meal. Then, in a bookshop around Harvard Square, Peter picked out a new book on The King by a man reputed to be the world authority on Elvis's music, a man whom Peter had met. I looked at the shelves, thick with books on the dead King. After that, Peter and I parted. In a few days, he would return to Iowa and begin teaching his course.

Peter was cautiously up-beat about America. In Africa, he had, like so many Third World writers, written essays against American cultural imperialism. Initial impressions when he first arrived from Africa were not much better. He had been, after all, an alien Asian. He spoke often about the insularity of American taste in literature; how Americans were convinced that American writers were better because America was better. But in Iowa, Peter – Goan and Asian, formerly of Uganda, Africa, now living in the heart of America – had found a kind of acceptance and even fame in his connection to Elvis, one of America's icons.

❖

In America, I read the *New York Times* each day and the *Boston Globe* on Sundays. There were also a number of different local newssheets in Cambridge, dealing with anything from local politics to second-hand goods, outdoor activities and gay meeting groups. On TV, there was cable: the three established networks, newcomer Fox and dozens of others, the most important of which, in terms of serious news, was the Public Broadcasting System, or PBS. Through the computer, via Nexis, the news information service, I reached out to hundreds of papers and news services.

The knowledge that was available to me was varied and voluminous. I felt like a child at a fun-fair. Dazzled by all the lights and attractions but getting overfed on information, like eating candy-floss and all types of foods that might not sit well together. When Vice-President

Gore talked about constructing an information super-highway for America, I felt that – plugged into this grid of paper, airwaves and electronics – I already had a taste of what it would be like. Each time I went to Harvard Square, I would think of it.

Near to the entrance to the T, the underground train system, there were two magazine stores: Out of Town Tickets and, across the street, Nina's. Both carried every magazine you could name, and more you had never heard of: from *Quilt* to *Foreign Affairs*, from porn to computer mags. Out of Town Tickets also carried daily newspapers from across the world, from Latin America and the Caribbean to China (although there was no *Straits Times*). It was like the information highway made concrete and put on the racks.

I would always make it a point to browse. I settled on the *Utne Reader* as a favourite, a bi-monthly magazine that selected the most interesting articles from magazines that were not in the mainstream of the media. But often I bought nothing more than the local newspaper. It was just the feeling of having access to so much information.

The contrast to Singaporean media – at that time, with just one newspaper company, one TV broadcasting company, limited access to Internet and few good bookstores – was real. Singaporeans are right to expect more from the media, particularly as Singapore may be one of the countries best equipped in technology and hardware. Key differences are the ideal of freedom of information, and the free press that Americans accept and even tout as their heritage.

The American media is proud of that tradition of independence and freedom. They see themselves as a "Fourth Estate", to check on the abuse of the other arms of government, particularly the Executive. In this, they have been disdainful of the media in many developing countries. Any press that advocates responsibility or sees themselves as contributing to the development of their country, is criticised as being controlled government agents. They brook no limitation on the freedom of speech and, therefore, the freedom of the press. This has its admirable aspects. But a free press is not a neutral and unbiased press. Each news provider has a bias, a viewpoint. Some are more liberal, others lean towards conservatism; almost all are, in the end, pro-American. Critics of the American press point, for example, to the stereotyping of racial minorities and to made-up stories, even in prestigious newspapers. The *New York Times*, perhaps the most influential newspaper in the country, is regularly criticised in a newsletter, *In Our Times*, that is dedicated to pointing out its errors and biases.

Another criticism was voiced by Nobel prize winner and intellectual Noam Chomsky. He believes that the media is manufacturing consent and opinions, rather than accurately reporting and revealing them. Chomsky claims, for example, that in the 1970s there was a conspiracy among the press to keep quiet the Indonesian seizure of East Timor. History too suggests that the American press can be less than unbiased. There is a strand pointed out by Daniel Boorstein and other historians that some call "boosterism". This originates from the days when new towns sprouted on the American continent and competed to attract settlers and business, deploying a newspaper to sing its praises to the point of propaganda. That element is not a relic of those early days of the press in America. It can still be seen in coverage of the Gulf War and other causes which Americans want to believe in and uphold to the point of shutting out other views. The free press in America does not aim for neutrality. What it offers, rather, is choice.

Choice is also the reply it gives to the critics of the Western press. Americans strongly believe the answer to mistakes and biases in their press cannot be put right by allowing governmental control. Rather, they seek to combat freedom of speech with more freedom. So, for example, if someone who is standing for election is criticised by a radio station, he or she can ask for equal air time to defend themselves. With such measures, Americans hope to create a market place of ideas, where the one who can convince more listeners will prevail.

That seems fair enough at first glance. Looking more closely, however, it still seems the system is more free than fair. The right of reply, to return to our example, does not prevail in the newspapers. Unlike radio and TV, they have no obligation to publish rebuttals and replies. This discrepancy is based mainly on historical roots. The press, unlike TV and radio, arose before government was strong enough to apply and enforce such controls. And it has fought off any attempts to impose them now.

The idea of freedom of speech, moreover, may also be elusive because the media is dominated by a handful of giants: the major TV stations and the newspapers of repute. It is not government censorship if these media ignore those with certain views. But the practical result is that those who are ignored then have little or no means to make their views known to a wider audience. People with such opinions, like Chomsky, are left to the marginal, alternative magazines and newsletters such as *Z* or *Mother Jones*. These alternative outlets, while interesting, have a much smaller circulation than the big boys. Conversely, money can literally buy freedom of speech, especially in politics. Enormous sums are spent on election campaigns and much of it is devoted to buying up TV air-time. Those who can afford more small-box exposure – like tycoon Ross Perot in his 1992 presidential bid – can win notice and votes much more easily.

The American market place of ideas is like a large forum with different stalls set up to attract customers. Some purveyors of ideas have bigger store-fronts, louder speaker systems and, perhaps, lucky draw prizes. They attract many more customers than the smaller stalls, regardless of the quality of their product. The market place is not an orderly or equal trading floor. People and ideas jostle and shout for attention. It can be confusing and a little loud. No one is a neutral adviser to the would-be buyer. But, if you shop carefully, listen discerningly, there is a bargain somewhere, the right thing for the right price, something you want and need. At that time in America, this seemed true. And that, for all its other faults and inconveniences, is the enduring promise of the American media.

"You going to buy that?" Ken asked me when we were in Nina's newsstand. It was a copy of the *Want Ads*, a weekly compilation of classified advertisements that offered everything from cars and used furniture to stamps and holiday homes.

"Ya, I get it once in a while. That's where Jin spotted the travelling trunk that's in our living room."

"Sure," Ken said. "I like to read it too. Lots of stuff in there."

"What is it?" There was something in his voice that made me ask.

"It's just whether you want to buy it here."

"Here? At Nina's, you mean?"

"Yeah, haven't you noticed?"

"No, what?"

"They're bigots," he whispered. "They don't like Chinese. Every time I come here, the guy will chat with everyone else who lines up to pay him. But he never says anything to me. Even when I say something, he just doesn't reply. Zip. Maybe I'm just over-sensitive but it seems odd to me. So I never buy anything here anymore. But go ahead. You go ahead and get that."

"No, it's OK."

"No, like I said, maybe I'm just too sensitive."

"Maybe you are, but maybe you aren't. So I'll buy it at Out of Town Tickets."

"You sure?"

"It's just across the street."

"That's true," my friend said. "That's one thing about America. Choice."

caning, crime and politics

caning
michael fay

"When will the West understand, or try to understand, the East? We Asiatics are often appalled by the curious web of facts and fancies which has been woven concerning us."

Kakuzo Okakura, *The Book of Tea*

"HI!" The American voice boomed with enthusiasm. "Look into the camera and tell me where you're from!"

"Singapore," I answered, less loudly.

Farmer Doone smiled, one eye still glued to the viewing piece on the video camera strapped to his shoulder. He had no idea where Singapore was. I could tell it from his face, from the part unobscured by the equipment. But, like most Americans in the Mid-West, he was a good host. His big, hairy hand gripped mine, firmly, briefly. "Welcome to our farm. Welcome to Iowa. The heart of America."

The Doone farm stretched as far as the eye could see. The white fence marked off the small road that ran along part of the land, towards town. But nowhere was there sight of another house, another family. The farm grew corn. Acres and acres of it, a genetically-engineered, high-yield variety that was dried and used for animal feed. Farmer Doone's son was out among the corn stalks at the wheel of a huge combine harvester, made by the John Deere factory, headquartered in a nearby town. He looked out through the glass-windowed cabin and waved at us. The machine rumbled on, its noise deafening; bits of corn stalk flying around us in a dusty whirl.

The Doones had acres of soya bean too, a mile or so further down. They also kept some cows, and pigs in sheds nearest the house. The pigs were pink and huge, lying on mud-smeared cement floors, under aluminium roofs. The Doones used to milk the cows to produce ice-cream, the best in the area. But now they left it to another business, buying milk from other producers.

After our tour of the land and farm buildings, when we returned to the house, it seemed small. In the living room, there was an old three-seater couch on which the Doones, big people, fitted comfortably. The curtain drapes had tassels. The carpets were mock Persian, manufactured in Belgium. The dining table was compressed wood with an oak veneer, a replica of an old style, shiny with Lemon Pledge. There was a piano, three glass-faced cabinets crammed with knick-knacks. The kitchen was less middle-class, more linoleum.

A farm in Iowa is part of the Mid-West, America's bread basket, the vast middle that provides mountains of wheat, corn and other grain to feed this country. It is a mythical land. The quiet farms and the flat plains to which so many Americans, now in the cities, trace their family roots. As more and more people leave the farms and small towns, that relationship is increasingly distanced. Farms have also become large corporations – agri-business, not agriculture. But not for the Doones. They lived on here, running the farm that had been their family's for generations. For some time still, this will be what Americans picture when they think of the average American: Iowa and farmer Doone. This is the country's heartland.

After we settled in and began eating, Farmer Doone left the table and came back out of another room with an old atlas. "Where is your country?" he asked. When I pointed out Singapore on the map, he remarked on its size. Or rather the lack of it. Sixteen miles from north to south? He shook his head in disbelief. He travelled further than that each time he went into town. But three million people? He sucked through his teeth lightly. That was more than Cedar Rapids, the nearest big city to his farm. Singapore was a long way away and very different, Farmer Doone nodded. As we ate dinner, his questions about Singapore continued. He knew we did not live in huts, but how did we fit so many people in such a small island? What food did our farmers grow? Did we eat turkey?

I ate and answered him slowly. He found the idea of so many apartments almost as alien as thatched huts; the vision of a country without farmers, distinctively unsettling. Gathered around the table, others of the large

Doone family chipped in with their own questions. Mrs Doone asked about Chinese silk and national dress. The grandson was happy to hear we had McDonald's. His son had heard of Singapore Airlines and hoped to fly it one day.

No one really knew Singapore. Until the atlas was brought out, they did not even know where it was. The Doones were not alone in this. It was not the fact that Singapore was small. Many Americans remain ignorant of even much, much larger Indonesia. Few have ever been to Asia. Most have never left America; those living in Iowa and other more rural states may not even have crossed state lines.

The Mid-West is a place where you can drive for 12 hours and never see much more than the ripening fields of wheat and corn. The people too seem similarly uniform; almost 98 per cent White. Most have been settled in America for many generations. A Jew or Black may be cause for comment, even if no one remarks on it from a sense of politeness. Any Asian is assumed to be foreign.

My use of English made me understandable. But it did not allow me to blend in; it became a source of double confusion. "You are a foreigner? But you speak English so well!" This innocent remark repeated itself many times, from many different people. It meant many things. On one occasion, the remark was passed by a girl with an Italian surname. She had black wavy hair that she wore long, with loose curls, and an olive tone to her complexion. She looked like one of the subsidiary figures in a Botticelli painting.

"How long has your family been in America?" I asked.

"My grandfather came from the old country," she said.

"Do you write in Italian, or speak it?"

"No. Just a few words."

"My family has been in Singapore and Malaya for five generations. Before that we were somewhere in Southeast Asia, out of China. We dealt with the British, were part of their Empire, and Singapore chose to keep English."

Why was it not strange that she, after a shorter time, should give up Italian for English, while everyone continued to wonder why I spoke English? There was no answer to such a question: just a polite pause in the conversation, like the presence of something that cannot be talked about. It was because I looked Asian, Chinese. Because of the colour of my skin. We both knew that, but no one said anything. We talked about something else.

In 1990, when I was in Iowa, Farmer Doone's friendly but blank response was more or less typical. So was the Italian girl's question. Americans had very little awareness of Singapore, if any at all. I had been to the heart of America. And it had detected my foreignness, like an alien particle in a body to be isolated by white cells. The old remark – "Singapore? Where? Is it in China?" – summed up our place in the common imagination of America. In just four years, this was to change dramatically.

A debate began to brew between East and West. This did not concern the old shouting match between communism and capitalism. On that, Singapore and its ASEAN neighbours had quite clearly been on America's side. Now, it was about other things: free and fair trade; what rights citizens had; why tropical forests and certain animal species had to be preserved; how to govern. It was about whether Asia, rapidly growing in economic importance, would be more or less like America; whether we would like America and whether they would like us. Allegiances in this new debate were more mixed among the different nations of Asia.

In this discussion, Singapore was not quiet. A number of Singaporeans were seen to be spokesmen promoting concepts that differed from America's; a system of belief some Western academics labelled "the Singapore school". Shortly before I left for the USA, there was a conference in Singapore about American and Asian perspectives on economy and democracy. A Singaporean at the conference spoke against the American system of free press. He accused it of arrogance, of hypocrisy and of doing more harm than good. He was dressed in an elegant suit but his words were pungent and somewhat sardonic. An American journalist put aside his prepared speech and replied in equally combative tone. He was emotional and scathing. By the end, the two protagonists seemed not to be talking to each other. Their dialogue had ended in a tense, brooding silence.

For an academic, intellectual exchange in the quiet, pastel surroundings of a five-star hotel, this collision was akin to a blood-fight. In the audience, part of me was uneasy with the strident tones the Singaporean used. It seemed an unbecoming voice to use on a foreign guest; an unAsian way of putting forward an Asian point of view. But another part of me accepted many points in his argument, and actually delighted in having someone tell off those Americans who seem so often to tell other people what to do.

But these arguments at conferences and hotel function rooms do not bring headlines. They do not evoke curiosity among the general public on either side of the Pacific, no matter how interesting they are. Some articles in foreign news magazines, like the *New Yorker*, went some way towards that. Typically, these remarked on our cleanliness and economic success while chaffing at our system of fines and campaigns. Some went on to talk about political detainees; one even called Singapore a "City of Fear". Still, in the heartland of America, nothing stirred. In the mind of farmer Doone, no recognition or attention flickered to life. For that, and for Singapore to be fixed on the map of the American mind, it took an 18-year-old boy, a Mercedes and a rotan.

❖

An American classmate stopped me in the corridor of the law school one day in spring. We were in the same seminar the previous fall, and he knew where I was from.

"Your country whips people?"

"No."

"That's what I just heard on the radio. Singapore is whipping some American kid for spray-painting someone's car."

"What? I haven't heard."

"Yeah, well, that's what the radio said. Is it like the Middle East laws? There, they cut off your hand if you are caught stealing."

"No, we don't cut off hands or whip people."

"But that's what the radio said."

"It could be a caning. You can be caned for some crimes like rape in Singapore. That's in addition to jail."

"And spray-painting a car?"

"Vandalism? I've got to check it up. Maybe there's caning for that too."

"How's that different from a whipping?"

I looked at my classmate. He had always been fair and soft-spoken in our classroom discussions. He was interested in China and we had talked a few times, sometimes arguing as lawyers are meant to, but on other occasions finding a good deal in common. But when I looked at him after this brief exchange, just before we parted ways for our different classes, I realised that he did not know me. Nor I, him.

And that was the first time I heard about the Michael Fay affair. It was not the last. I found out the facts of the matter from the *Boston Globe*, the city newspaper. Then I followed up on Nexis, the news update service, looking up other news sources all over the country and counter-checking them against *Straits Times* reports. That evening, I went down to the basement of the Lewis Library at the university. There, the legislation of countries starting from "P" to "Z" were kept, together with other legal commentaries and books. The shelves for Singapore, just before South Africa, surrendered the familiar red files that compiled all our country's legislation. Flipping through, I found the offence and the compulsory sentence of caning. It was an odd context to learn of the crime and punishment that was defended and almost taken for granted back home: in the corridors of America's best-known law school and one with a history of liberalism.

In America, there is a belief in punishing the crime, not the criminal. The ethos is to rehabilitate criminals, whether in jail or by making them undergo social counselling. Faced with aberrant behaviour, liberals will almost always put education forward as the answer, not the physical punishment of the cane. Connected to this is a tendency to emphasise the root causes of crime in society: the lack of opportunity, education and guidance among the poor. Part of me has an empathy for such approaches to social problems.

Another part of me, bred in Singapore, believes in hard and practical measures. For crime, police. For criminals, punishment. I was not alone in this belief in America. A growing number had begun to see such approaches as the solution to the problems of crime in the country. In that atmosphere, almost every politician promised to get tough on crime; they knew that this was what the public wanted to hear.

At about the time the Fay affair came up, even as he asked Singapore to reconsider the sentence, President Clinton put forward a Crime Bill with measures to get tough on crime. One of these was to refuse parole to criminals acquitted for a third serious offence. Taking a cue from this country's favourite pastime, baseball, the proposal was for "Three strikes and you're out." Or rather, in jail, permanently. Although popular with many, others attacked it as being too tough, and for being misdirected. The lawyer that Clinton first appointed as deputy attorney-general, Philip Heymann, argued against such laws. He urged for that liberal panacea – doing more to tackle the social causes of crime. But his arguments never got a fair hearing amidst the increasingly loud calls for urgent, tough measures against crime. So Heymann resigned from Clinton's administration and returned to the ivy-covered law school whence he and his liberal ideas came: Harvard.

In this context, Singapore's sanction against one young American unwittingly became a piece in a much larger American puzzle. Liberals would not brook any argument in favour of the sentence in Singapore, especially since it was not just the figurative three strokes the president had proposed but actual ones with a rotan. On the other hand, surveys conducted around the country consistently showed a greater acceptance than expected. A call-in survey of 23,000 people showed that 53 per cent favoured whipping and other harsh sentences as an acceptable deterrent to crime in the USA. In Fay's hometown of Dayton, Ohio, the editor of the local newspaper reported that many had called in who "were not at all sympathetic". In a Los Angeles newspaper, readers had written in to support the Singapore action. Stated reasons ranged from the immediate – "I am tired of seeing graffiti in our city" – to the expansive – "The bottom line is that Singapore has a criminal justice system that works and we (Americans) do not."

Fed by American concerns and comments, the Fay story quickly spread on TV programmes and in the newspapers. I read up the facts and the law. I also talked to people, getting earfuls of opinion one way or the other. Especially in the human rights seminar that I attended at the law school: Andy, a young Jewish man with a head of bushy curls and with a senator as an uncle, who believed America had a duty to intervene in Haiti; Mumbi, from Africa, who felt that America had no right interfering in any place; Kerry, a Canadian, who focused on women's issues; Drew, a young African-American from the south, whose idea of human rights was shaped by how it could help in the ghettos of America; Xiao Bing, a Chinese national who used to teach in a state-run institute of foreign policy; and Ying, a quiet young woman from Taiwan, who wanted American-style democracy in her country. Among these, and others in the seminar, we always had interesting discussions on a whole range of human rights issues, taking in differing perspectives. Even if we did not always agree with what we heard, we listened to each other. But little of this prepared me for the events that were soon to pull me close to the epicentre of the controversy.

❖

The "Larry King Show" called late one afternoon. They were running a show about Michael Fay with his father and an American attorney. Would I be willing to go on the show to give a Singaporean perspective? I was not their first choice. They had asked the Singapore embassy in Washington DC but they had refused. My name had been recommended by someone and they had traced me through the law school. Would I appear on CNN, live in the studio? An appearance fee could be negotiated. They could do a satellite patch from Boston. Flying me out to be in the studio with Larry and the others would, however, be their preference. If I was short of time, this could be done on the day of the interview itself with a return flight, straight after the show.

The producer who called from the show gushed forth with his explanations while I stood in our apartment on the quiet, dead-end street, just back from a refreshing walk around the neighbourhood. I looked across at Jin Hua who was drinking a cup of tea and raised my eyebrows. They wanted to know more about my background and I told them. What were my views on the Fay matter? They wanted to know for the programme. I answered this too. I replied that, for various reasons, Singaporean laws should prevail over American objections. You sound like the right person, they said. Otherwise, they were going to ask another Singaporean in America, Francis Seow, a man who had once stood for elections but was now wanted on tax charges. Would I do it? I asked for their number and said I would call back in an hour or so, after considering it.

Jin Hua's counsel was not to do it. When two sides were entrenched, it was a difficult, indeed dangerous, to have a position in-between; like the grass in that old Asian adage about buffaloes fighting. I wanted to find out why our embassy had declined the invitation from the show. I spoke to someone I knew at the embassy. He explained that the hope was that the "Larry King Show" could not go ahead if there was no Singaporean voice. This seemed unlikely; the show had already been advertised on CNN. Other news shows had also carried segments on it, and the King show would not be left behind. I told him about their offer to me and the possibility that they might otherwise ask Francis Seow. There was a brief silence on the line. He would get back to me. I drank tea with Jin Hua and waited. They called back to say that there were no objections if I went on the show, provided that it was made very clear that I was voicing my personal opinions and not those of the government.

The "Larry King Show" called again. This time we had a longer chat about my views. Was Asia, they asked, standing up to America? I did not think that this issue was about Asia as a whole, I replied, nor was I a spokesman for it. Was caning always justified? I was not saying that caning was right for all offences, only that it was the law of Singapore and had, moreover, been enforced without any objection until an American was to be caned. Was the American reaction justified? I pointed to the surveys that suggested there was support among many citizens, in contrast to the media coverage that was mostly biased against the punishment. I complained that the media was often factually inaccurate – showing ridiculous "re-enactments" that depicted caning being carried out with a six-foot long wooden pole and playing footage of public whippings in an Islamic country. There was a silence on the phone. They would call me back again, they said, after discussing the matter.

When they called, it was to tell me that they had re-considered the situation. They wanted a person with an opinion that was wholly in favour of the punishment and about Asia's right to stand up to America. Or they would have a Singaporean on who was clearly against what his government was doing. Again, they mentioned Francis Seow. They did not really feel that the points I'd made about the media coverage were relevant. Nor did they want to focus on crime in America. What the show really wanted was a spokesperson for the Singapore government, or a critic willing to say that their government was wrong to cane Fay. I was neither: I was not appointed to the first role, and unwilling to perform the latter.

I spoke to the embassy again. They were still considering whether to take part in the show. I encouraged them to make the case for Singapore. Otherwise, the producers would find a Singaporean willing to un-make it for a few minutes on CNN. With all the calls over, I sat down for another cup of tea with Jin Hua, in our apartment, looking out onto our empty back yard. I did not know what happened immediately afterwards. But the next day, Ambassador S.R. Nathan, Singapore's man in Washington, went on the "Larry King Show".

In the aftermath, more offers from different media came in. One, a rather sensational magazine-format news show, got my name from someone at the Singapore Economic Development Board. They wanted me to go around a bad urban sector in an American city and comment on the sense of dirt, danger and crime from a Singaporean perspective. Another, referred to me by an American human rights organisation in Washington, wanted me to comment on the "authoritarian" practices in Singapore. I declined both invitations. From my position in-between, it was clear to me that the media in

America had made up their mind about the issue. I was interested in exchanging views but not in mouthing opinions tailored to fit preconceived conclusions.

It took the *New York Times* to stir me out of this silence. It was an article by William Safire, a well-known and reputable columnist who had once been a speech writer for President Nixon. I read him regularly; sometimes agreeing, at other times disagreeing, always preferring his column on language to politics. Safire's column, published on 7 April 1994, proceeded from language to attack Singapore's caning of Fay. From a dictionary definition, he argued that pain was "torture" and that caning was "torture" since it inflicts pain. Torture was uncivilised – like the Nazis or like Saddam Hussein's persecution of the Kurds. Safire described Singapore as a "dictatorship" and a "lawless state". He put aside two difficulties facing his argument. An American who agreed with the punishment was thoughtless, characterised as "a sap on the street". The fact that America has the death penalty – which some human rights advocates also see as "torture" or "cruel and inhumane punishment" – was also blithely dismissed. Safire saw it as "not germane; that retributive justice by lethal injection is painless".

The insults to my country stung. The sloppy, biased arguments irritated me. That evening I faxed a reply to the *New York Times*, and mailed off a copy as well. In my reply, I pointed out Safire's simplistic definitions: he mixed up pain with torture while ignoring the death penalty and the deplorable condition in many American jails; he had ignored the United Nations convention on torture that allowed "lawful sanction", such as the

Singapore court's decision against Fay. I suggested it was disingenuous to raise the Nazis and the Kurdish issue when there was no racial or ethnic persecution in Fay's case. I accused him of undemocratically ignoring the opinion of his fellow citizens – labelled as "sap(s) on the street" – who supported Singapore, perhaps out of a genuine anger with crime in their own country. I also said that it smacked of imperialism for America to intervene for one of their citizens when it had never before cared about any of the others who had received the same punishment.

When I wrote my letter, I hoped but did not expect it to be published. The American media do not always grant a right of reply. I was right. My reply was not published. No correspondence explained its rejection or even acknowledged its receipt. Freedom of speech in this case meant I was free to write and they were free to ignore it. There was no equal access. Without it, some like Safire were freer to speak than others, like me. The American media had spoken and, having convinced itself, seemed not to be listening to other points of view.

In the following days, the *New York Times* would ask American industry to pull out of Singapore, for tourists to avoid visiting the country and for everyone to deluge the embassy by phone, fax and letter. One article even pondered, not disapprovingly, if some elements might seek vengeance against Singaporeans in America. That suggestion – amplified in a *Straits Times* commentary – resulted in my mother calling long-distance. "Tell people you're from Malaysia," was her advice.

I did not. I carried on saying I was from Singapore. But I stopped seeking to defend what my country had done. Not from fear of American thugs masquerading under the guise of human rights; there simply was no need to be defensive. In conversation after conversation, when it was brought up, Americans took up that task themselves. Some did so because they were fed up with crime. Others, perhaps the majority, did so because they felt America should respect the laws of another country. Even if someone present disagreed, the debate proceeded without much attention to what I or other Singaporeans said. Among any group of Americans, most had heard and each had an opinion, one way or the other. It was not a conversation about Singapore, but one about America. It was also a conversation in which both sides seemed to speak, without listening to the other.

At a small gathering in a university group, a Singaporean said simply and flatly that she was all for it. Caning works, she said shortly. She was convinced. How about the pain? someone asked. The Singaporean girl reiterated her conviction with a smile: it works. No matter what arguments anyone brought up, that was her reprise, her bottom line. After a while, the discussion ended. One of the Americans present told me he could not decide if her certainty was a sign of strength or of smugness.

A week later, I lunched with various Harvard students who had an interest in human rights. Andy Levin, my classmate from the human rights seminar, came up to me. Andy launched into a diatribe about Fay. He focused on allegations that those who were "whipped" would go into shock. On that point, I felt it necessary to distinguish between whipping and caning, and to point to the presence of medical doctors. But he talked on and on, about whipping and shock, airing a dozen or so mistakes of fact. He was not speaking to me, I realised, but to the others at the table. He was also not listening, smug in his sense of righteousness.

"You're not listening to me, Andy." I said it without raising my voice. It stopped him for a minute and he turned to look across at me. "But that's all right," I continued. "I've been ignored by much more famous Americans than you."

❖

The four of us were throwing an American football around; three pre-school kids and one slightly over-grown example, just having fun. I was playing with Karen and Linus's children in the yard. After they left, Helen, one of our neighbours, called. The yard was shared by all four apartments. The tasks of mowing the lawn, liming the soil, raking the leaves: these were shared, as were the joys of using it for a BBQ or picnic. Helen, however, asked us not to play again on the lawn. She was con-cerned the grass would be damaged.

She invited herself down to our apartment to tell us this. We sat at the table by the window, overlooking the green lawn. I looked out as she voiced her objection; not to ignore her. Helen was not the kind of neighbour you could ignore. She had told the neighbour across the street not to play music so loudly. She had told off another neighbour for driving too quickly along the narrow dead-end street. More than that, she had told us, being part of the neighbourhood, of these requests, to solicit our express or tacit support. Both offenders had ceased their anti-social behaviour, for which I admit we were grateful. So when she made the requests, it seemed not just Helen's whim but the sentiment of the small community along Winslow Street.

Now she sat in our living room and waited for our agreement. I had little doubt that Helen would report our offence to others for their disapproval, if she had not already. But I looked out and the sun was bright and the grass seemed unmarked by our little game. "No," I replied. "We will continue to play. It's just a little fun – a little throwing and catching with three small children, not the Harvard football team. And that's what back yards are for."

Helen stopped sipping her tea. Her face tightened and the lines above her narrow upper lip seemed to grow deeper. She insisted. The conversation devolved into an account of who did what for the garden and who had stayed longer here; a petty squabble was threatened. But over tea, we compromised. We could throw and catch the ball but we would not run too fast or too hard on the grass. Helen went on about the care the grass needed. She was not happy with the compromise, but could not but accept it. "Ridiculous," Jin Hua said when she had gone off.

Something in this brought the Fay matter again to my mind. It was still in the news at the time. I held onto my belief that, whatever moral stand people took on caning, America had no right to interfere. But I was also chastened by my counter-reaction. My indignation was in danger of breeding its own blind nationalism: that anything and everything Singapore did was right. To me, those sentiments were no better than the American stand. One jingoism bred its opposing vehemence. I tried to look for a common humanity in it all, something that was truer than the trumpets that call men to fight for nations, either with guns or words. "Good fences make good neighbours" – that's what the American poet Robert Frost wrote. He may be correct. There is a streak in Americans which leads some of them to mind other people's business. Perhaps it is part of the puritan, missionary zeal that started this country. Perhaps it also explains their vigilance and insistence on their rights to privacy – it is a counter-reaction, a fence, against other people's prying. Without privacy or demarcating fence, my American neighbour had intruded on our enjoyment of a simple, occasional game. Or, to see things from her point of view, we had intruded on her enjoyment of an empty yard.

A compromise had been reached. But, honestly, I only agreed since, living next door, our relationship would have to continue. On her part, Helen was never completely satisfied. There was always a chill in her voice after that time I first said no. There was something in this about the controversy over the American's caning. Something about fences, other people's business and also about universal values and understanding – not smugness – on both sides. Good fences make good neighbours: even in a global village, this seemed some-thing worth remembering.

criminal
elements

A TALE OF TOO MANY CITIES   One night, coming home late from the university library, I drove into our dead-end street to see someone standing in my neighbour's yard, digging with a shovel. One of the street lights was out and I could not see who it was. It was near 11; not a usual time for gardening. I should have minded my own business and gone straight inside. America has generated enough tales of horror – celluloid and real – to make discretion the safer option in the face of strange events. But there was something that made me pause. I saw a tall woman with long white hair, in a white robe. She was digging a hole for the large black rubbish bag next to her.

"Edna?" I called out. I recognised the figure as one of two elderly sisters who lived next door. We had spoken briefly whenever we met; she was too friendly, I was sure, to be some sort of axe murderer caught in the act of hiding the evidence of her latest victim. She was startled when I called. She hadn't seen me walking up and did not recognise my voice.

It had been a bad day, she explained; a windy fall day, cold enough to remind her that winter was coming on. She and her sister had spent all day indoors. When evening came, they could not find one of their cats. They looked around for her when darkness came. The wind had been so strong, they found a piece of marble garden furniture toppled over, on top of the cat. Edna's sister, extremely fond of the cat, was distraught. She couldn't sleep until it was decently buried. That explained what Edna was doing with the shovel at night. She had started after dinner and wasn't anywhere near finished.

Edna was a hearty, firm New England woman. She and her sister walked regularly for exercise, in their grey jogging pants and Nikes. But she was in her 60s or 70s and I made the offer to take over. So now it was me, an Asian man standing in someone else's yard near midnight, working away with a shovel to bury a cold, stiff body. But no one came by, no neighbours and no police car, and I did not have to attempt an explanation. Edna went back into her house for just a while, and returned with a cup of hot tea, standing by me until I finished. When I did, we said goodnight and I went into my home and told the story to Jin, who laughed. The next morning, Edna and her sister came by with a pretty pot of poinsettia, dressed up in Christmas ribbons, to thank me. From that day, the two sisters never failed to greet us and chat when we met on the street, going out or coming in.

That was where I lived, the kind of neighbourhood it was. It was a safe place, far away from the gunshots and urban crime that newsreels constantly reported. Safe enough – so it seemed – that you could stop in the middle of the night and ask a person with a shovel what she was burying in the back yard. No robberies. No car vandals. No drugs. That was the tale of our neighbourhood in Cambridge.

❖

There are other tales of cities. Washington DC is America's capital, which I visited as a guest panellist for a symposium at the American University. The topic was human rights and the professors were knowledgeable, assertive. One advised the former Communist countries in Eastern Europe about their constitutions. Another had taken on cases against repressive Central American governments. They talked about freedom and politics across the world, shifting their gaze from one foreign country to another, dispensing wisdom. They were confident people, accustomed to being listened to. I met them the day before the symposium for a brief discussion, then I left for some sight-seeing.

Herman Schwartz, the law professor who was my host, was helpful. He put me up in a comfortable and convenient hotel near the university and within easy reach of the city's underground trains – the best I've used abroad. Herman gave me a lift back to the hotel in a car strewn with so many things there was hardly space to sit. I told him about my plans to see the city.

"You'll love it," he said, nodding so his heavy spectacles slid further down his large nose. His gravelly voice took on almost a wistful tone. "There's no city like it in the world. When I was in Eastern Europe, they asked me about more than our constitution, which is what I went to advise them on. They asked me what our cities were like, how we lived, what we ate and did. They were so hungry to know things. It was all those decades, you see. All that time that they couldn't travel and see what the rest of the world was like, what America was like. You couldn't travel, not unless you were someone in the Party. That was why the Wall came down, you know. Not because of the economics or the weapons. Not that. The Wall came down because they wanted to know what was on the either side." Herman nodded his balding head slowly and pursed his lips at the thought.

After that and until the car was at the entrance of my hotel, he told me about places to see. Herman spoke as if he was dictating a letter to a rapid-fire stenographer. But I got a rough idea of things. I set out for the centre where Washington DC has concentrated the Lincoln Memorial, Capitol Hill, the Washington monument and the White House. Gleaming white, set amidst wide avenues and grass verges. Grand monuments, appropriate for the president and congress of the world's sole superpower. That first night, I walked from point to point, taking in the sights and the crisp night air until I was hungry and late for dinner. But I had not seen everything.

There was, I had heard, another Washington DC. In the southeast and other areas, reports came of violence, gangs and drugs, broken homes and poverty. From such places, the frightening statistics emerged which made America's capital also one of the cities with the highest murder toll. "DC", some say, stands for Death Capital. Early next afternoon, after another short meeting at the university, I headed out to those troubled areas.

"You want to go where?" The cab driver turned around and shot the question when I named a street in a troubled sector of DC. "You must be from out of town," he concluded. "I don't go there. Nobody does." He cheerfully admitted that his refusal to take me, a paying passenger, to that area was against the rules, technically. He had good reason, however. "Too many drivers get beat-up," he said, without looking around. "Their cars get beat-up. Some drivers are stabbed. Friend of mine took a fare down there. The guy ran out the door without paying. He was so damn angry, my friend runs after him. He ran until he heard the gunshot. Then, he stopped and just turned back. It's not worth it, you know? Anyway, when he gets back to the cab, the four tyres are missing. Can you beat that? Shit! Me, I just don't go there no more. It's not worth it. I'm just trying to make a living."

"You're not American, are you?" I nodded. My colour made that a natural guess among most Americans. "You're not used to this sort of thing, are you?" I nodded again. "It's OK. Me neither. It wasn't always like this. And, you know, even now, you never really get used to all this."

I asked about the police. They were either inept or corrupt, according to the cab driver; they closed both eyes to what was going on or even took charge of the drugs. I had read such newspaper reports about the DC police. I discounted these allegations; taxi drivers all over the world have grouses against governments, complaints that are prone to exaggeration. But I did not dismiss them as wholly untrue.

"So where do you wanna go?" he asked with a broad white-toothed grin, peering in the rear-view mirror. He smiled again when I told him to head for the Smithsonian Air and Space Museum. Instead of the city's problem areas, I went to the moon. I saw the technical expertise that got the Americans into space. I watched a show about our planet, simulated with state-of-the-art computers and visuals. I admired the museum itself; its great accumulation of knowledge. For an hour, I paused in wonder at American technology and power. Then, as I went out of the museum and into the city, under the darkening sky, I wondered again about the situation here on earth, close at hand.

The cab driver advised me in a serious tone not to stray in the area beyond the Supreme Court. The ultimate residence of law and order in America sits on the border of crime and chaos. "Crime used to be confined to one or two areas," he said when I left him. "Now, it can happen anywhere."

All over America, big cities are struggling. Tom Wolfe's *Bonfire of the Vanities* pivots on the simple mistake of a yuppie New Yorker taking a wrong turn into the wrong part of the city. That message of fear was well known before the bestseller and it certainly has sunk home since. In elections for the mayors of Boston and New York, crime, security and the cleaning-up of the city featured prominently. Almost all candidates identified these problems and promised to solve them, to get tough on crime. Just how to do that, in terms of strategy, administration and money, remains the question.

Death penalties and heavier sentences; more prisons, more police. Stricter gun control, less violence on TV and at the movies. Social work programmes, poverty alleviation and urban planning. Paying attention to school kids and their families. All these were just some of the problems and possible solutions which had been discussed in America. However, an agreement on the actual mix of these different elements had yet to arise. While that question remained, it was the mayors who had come and gone. Almost all the major cities had seen a change of leadership since the late 1980s. Again, Washington DC claimed the notorious spotlight: instead of catching others, DC's former mayor himself was caught in a drug bust. So while the newly-elected looked for solutions, individuals continued to vote with their feet. From the middle-class up, those who could afford it found suburbs and safe havens outside the city centre. Such individual solutions may be part of the community's problem.

The movement to the suburbs emptied the city, leaving it to the poor and the troubled. Crime is therefore not a problem in isolation. It is linked to the life and livelihood of neighbourhoods. Urban renewal that results in more suburbs, malls and the wholesale demolition of old areas can only create more problems. The answer that some proposed was a city life with 24-hour activity, in which neighbourhoods are alive and built on a human scale, with mixed areas of rich, middle-class and poor, and of different races. Much of this thinking can be traced to a book written more than 30 years ago: *The Death and Life of Great American Cities* by Jane Jacobs.

Jacobs, now in her 80s, with a distinguished head of silver hair, was not an urban planner, architect or politician; she never went to university. Her ideas remain controversial among many technocrats who actually plan and run the cities, but her commonsense approach to common problems is gaining wider acceptance. Despite this, Ms Jacobs has her doubts. "I think the United States is in a much worse way than people realise," she was quoted as saying. She observed that older cities were losing their industry and jobs, then their people and the sense of neighbourhood. "You have to have other (cities) coming up while those are going down. And I don't see that happening. And I don't see the suburbs taking their place. And I don't see the shopping malls taking the place of what downtowns did. So it's very, very worrisome."

I remembered these words. I had begun to worry a bit myself, walking through the night that comes early in fall. The parks and streets of Washington DC were dark and I thought again of the murder statistics. I have been in worse places, I told myself, remembering South American cities notorious for armed revolutions and bombings, and kidnapping and theft in Asian cities. But there was still something Singaporean in me that insisted that every street should be kept safe, at any time of night or day. Then I heard someone running towards me, feet crunching on the pebbly walkways between one monument and the next. I readied myself, tensed myself for fight or flight from a mugging or worse. Then the jogger went by, in a sweatshirt and track pants, with walkman strapped on and Nikes that glowed with every step he took.

Ahead of me, the monuments of the Capitol were lit, gleaming white and grand in the spotlights. I walked from the Washington Monument, that famous white obelisk, to the Lincoln Monument. In the park, police cordoned off an area while a helicopter landed. A government official rushed off to Congress or the White House to run the country. Above us, the moon the Americans have reached was bright but waning. Here, I thought, at least here and now, the city must be safe.

LAND OF A MILLION CHEAP GUNS Crime and guns are number one on the American charts. From movies with Arnie and Sly to TV series re-enactments like "True Crime" and constant news of the latest shootings – they are a source of entertainment. In the streets and homes of the city, they are a constant source of concern. More than 100 people a day are killed by firearms in America. The savage statistic includes some 50,000 children (since 1979). No one is exempt. Visitors and foreigners are, in fact, sometimes singled out. Tourists arriving in Miami have been identified by the license plates on their rental cars, followed and then killed for the money and luggage they have with them.

I received a call from a Singaporean acquaintance. He had been in the States for nearly ten years now and owned a collection of pistols and semi-automatic rifles.

"Just for self-protection," he advised, "get a gun."

And so I found myself in a gun shop. The giant moose head on the wall looked quizzically at me. So did the owner and shoppers in the gun store. All of them were men in their 40s, White. They were joking and telling stories. I felt I did not belong there.

America invented the cheap gun. Most of the shots fired during the American revolution had been from European-made muskets, hand-crafted and expensive. But at the end of the 18th century, an enterprising American, Eli Whitney, convinced the government that he could produce affordable guns. To do this, he got rid of the craftsman and introduced moulds and machines. Each part was interchangeable. In the process, Whitney introduced mass production, which he named the Uniformity system. Foreigners called it the American system. This system spawned the guns that conquered the West, like the famous Colt 45 revolver.

That was the one I asked for at the big display case. The store owner looked across at me a little warily. He did not joke with me or even smile. He bent down, unlocked the case and placed the gun on top, without ammunition. Its clatter was cold and crisp. It gleamed in the light. I hefted it, worked its mechanism. A classic piece.

"Too big for you," he said. "Old-fashioned and bulky."

"What would you suggest?" I asked him.

"Try this one."

He bent again and took another gun from the case. I picked it up. It was a smaller weapon, much lighter, matte black, sinister and sophisticated. He looked at me: "Just on the market two years ago. One of our bestsellers. Same calibre as the Colt. But it's light, hardly any recoil. Loads and fires like a dream." I pulled the trigger. It clicked on the empty chamber. It was that easy.

In America, there are about 1,200 manufacturers of firearms. They put out some 1.4 million handguns per year in a billion-dollar business. It has been a growth sector too. Since 1985, sales have jumped almost 100 per cent – new models flourishing while classics like the Colt have plummeted in sales. This would simply be a business statistic except for the fact that the rise in sales coincided with a 50 per cent jump in gun-related deaths.

Still, the gun industry has been able to lobby government effectively, with large funding and numbers of fervent grassroots supporters in the National Rifle Association. It is a constitutional right, they will remind you, to bear arms. It was the civilian-soldier, the American minuteman, who fought the Revolution. A heritage of militia, of guns and cowboys opening up the country and a constitutional provision combine with modern industry and lobbying to complicate any push for gun control.

When I was in America, the Brady Act came into force. It was pushed by James Brady, the former White House press secretary who was shot in the 1981 assassination attempt on President Reagan. Brady was now wheelchair-bound and a staunch advocate of the control of guns. Despite the publicity and sympathy that Brady earned, there was a seven-year fight to get the Bill approved. The new law, moreover, still did not prohibit gun ownership outright. It only required a five-day waiting period while the state ran a background check on the prospective buyer. If there was no criminal record or other reason to suspect the person, he or she could still purchase the gun.

It did not seem like much to me, used to strict gun laws. Yet, although modest, the Brady Act was the first gun control legislation for many years. Within the first few months, it was estimated to have prevented some 2,000 people from getting guns. Some believed that the Brady Act might have signalled the tide of public opinion and political action was turning in favour of regulation, against the gun lobby.

In the wake of the Brady Act, the Treasury re-classified semi-automatic shotguns so that buyers had to register their particulars. Other new legislation mooted national licensing. But many Americans still did not believe in regulation, especially the three million-plus citizens who belonged to the National Rifle Association. Those in favour of free access to guns were not finished. The battle over firearms – like *Rambo* and *Robocop* – had sequels.

"A bunch of paperwork. A damn nuisance," the store owner said when I brought up the Brady Act. "Damn politicians sit in Washington and pass laws that make no sense at all. I mean, if someone wants a gun, they're going to get it. Criminals don't shop here. They just get some Saturday night special off the streets." A couple of regular customers, trying out a semi-automatic rifle, looked across and nodded in agreement. One, wearing a plaid hunting cap, spoke up.

"Look at this state. Massachusetts has more gun laws than almost anywhere else. So, people do their shopping in New Hampshire. Less than two hours away, almost no rules."

"I just lose business," the store owner went on. "Now with Brady laws, people will just get it from Mexico or somewhere else. Smugglers will make the money, not me."

"Citizens will wait," the guy in the cap said, "but criminals will not."

"Why should we?" the other customer added, strapping on the rifle. "We have a right. It's in the Constitution."

"Yeah, Ed. It's impossible to disarm everyone. Maybe," he said turning back to me, "the solution would be for everyone to be armed, so criminals will think twice before attacking them."

"So, do you want it?"

I looked up blankly at him. A gun did not seem a decision I could make in just a few minutes. He sensed my uncertainty and suggested I try out some guns at a shooting range before deciding. He went back to his other customers, keeping one eye on me as I stood and considered the two handguns on the top of the case. On a nearby rack, I noticed cans of mace and pepper spray. The cans claimed they could immobilise would-be robbers and assailants from as much as 45 metres away; another form of self-defence, less bloody than guns. I shook my head at the store owner and pushed the guns away from me, back across the case. I reached over and took a pepper spray.

"It's for my wife."

That was true. The store owner nodded and turned away, smiling at another customer who strapped on a semi-automatic rifle. The moose head on the wall just stared straight ahead.

YOUNG AMERICANS Anna-Lise was 20. Lanky, with hair short as a boy's, she was dressed in sweatshirts and grungy jeans. She had twin earring holes in each ear and a love for art. By age and appearance, she qualified for America's Generation X, notorious for a stupid cynicism, selfishness, vacuous materialism and amorality. With her family, Anna-Lise had meandered across the USA, moving every three or so years when her father, an engineer, finished one project and took up another. Those movements had taken their toll. Anna-Lise scrunched up her lively face, remembering the pain of making new friends, of the rootlessness of all their coming and going.

"I was born in Thailand," she began, responding to my being Asian. "Not that I remember anything. I was too young. It was my father's first job, just after he and my Mum got married. We moved back to the States before I was even three. But Mum looks back on those days with such love that she always reminds me I was born in Asia. She says I could speak Thai. She says we had a maid there, a young girl who carried me around all the time and looked after me as if I was her own baby. Everyone used to call me the American child.

"When we came back, we moved to the Mid-West. Mum brought back rolls and rolls of Thai silk. Some she made into dresses but she gave me the rest for my wedding chest. When I was a teenager, she made me take the silk out once in a while to iron. She said it was to remind me of my birthright, whatever that means. Mum, of course, told everyone where I was born, and when I first started going to school, everyone called me the Asian kid. That wasn't good. I was trying to fit in, and kids made fun of me for being different – even something incidental, like where I was born."

It would have been easy from Anna-Lise's story to imagine a pattern of drift and delinquency as her family moved from one place to another. But Anna-Lise's young life defied that. She was a member of Generation X by age only. She didn't do drugs. Didn't watch "Beavis and Butt-head" on MTV, although she was in on the new music. She was not cynical, alienated or apathetic. Quite the reverse.

Anna-Lise was an anthropology student in a small college in Iowa. When she arrived in Iowa, she moved into a house for university students. Not only did she fit in, before long she had organised them into spear-heading the local efforts for recycling. Last summer, she volunteered to work in a housing project for the desti-tute in a bad neighbourhood of Chicago. Her group of young Americans did not terrorise the neighbourhood with senseless crimes and drugs. They re-built it, one unit after another, with hammer and nails. Anna-Lise was the chair of the college's honours year class project and editor of the department's journal. Such achievements suggested not a Generation X "dead-head", but a level-headed and socially-conscious citizen with a vegetarian-only, earthy stance.

Her 18-year-old sister, equally trendy in earrings and dress, studied in Colorado. There she helped run a nationwide student environmental coalition. When Anna-Lise arranged for us to meet, the talk did not centre around generational differences, Beavis or Butthead. Her sister told me about her involvement in the coalition and asked about the environmental problems in Asia. When we left, she scribbled out her e-mail address and asked me to keep in contact. Anna-Lise smiled. Her sister was a real contact-maker, an organiser and go-getter. She herself was more thoughtful and reflective, more laid-back.

Neither sister went to Woodstock II, the event that aimed to be the emblem of their generation. It drew over 250,000 people. On that Woodstock weekend, Anna-Lise was house-sitting a friend's dog and car while they were on holiday. Her sister was at an environmental grassroots conference in Chicago. "Woodstock's not my style," Anna-Lise said.

America invented youth culture. With rock-n-roll, jeans and teenage idols, it promoted the idea that it was good to be young. It gave the world Elvis, James Dean, Kurt Corbain and the image of restless youth, the rebel with or without a cause. It also promised young people that if they strived hard enough – however humble their backgrounds – they could do well and even be president, as Clinton himself had shown. That image and its promise have been exported to the world, along with music and MTV.

But recently, youth in America have gotten a lot of bad press. Newspapers told of street gangs pushing dope, teenagers killed in drive-by shootings, a ten-year old in Detroit who robbed and shot a woman, and a spreading virus of drugs, school drop-outs and HIV among those who would, in a different era and context, have been children. When three people were killed in the small town of Rochester, the shock was not because the small town seemed safe, unlike big cities. Nor that the victims were mother, father and their 11-year-old daughter. It was because the alleged killer was Gerry McCra, the family's 15-year-old son.

These problems seem more prevalent in poor, urban neighbourhoods and among minorities. There, street gangs with names like "La Familia" (The Family) and the "Latin Kings" fight for turf. Young men join in because they say the gangs give them the support and self-respect they crave and so become the family many never had. But troubled youth and the troubles they bring are also spreading to White teenagers and into once quiet towns, as the McCra killings showed. It became common wisdom that a culture of cynicism and violence prevailed among America's youth. The "X" of the Generation seemed to signify X-rated notoriety and perhaps an inferior quality, like a brand X of dubious value.

Against that background, I thought again of Anna-Lise and her sister. They seemed anomalies rather than examples. At first glance, Danny seemed more typical. He was a young African-American, not tall but broad and strong. He wore his hair short, almost shaved close to the scalp. He had a gentle, slow way of speaking. Otherwise, dressed in sweatshirt and jeans, he looked like a character out of *Boyz 'n the Hood* or another movie on the urban, troubled youth; someone you wouldn't like to meet in a dark alley.

Danny grew up in a poor area in the south. He didn't talk much about his family but, from what he said, I made out that his father was seldom around and gave little guidance. Chances were that he ended up in trouble with the law; one in every four African-American male youths is in prison, on parole or facing criminal charges. But he defied those odds. With encouragement and support of a mentor, Danny completed high school and went on to college. Along the way, he started a mentorship programme for street kids, passing on what he himself had received.

"We got a bad rep. People think we're trouble. If you're just driving or walking in the wrong area, the police are going to check on you. For no reason except that you're there. If you're young and Black, chances are you're just trying to survive. I made it somehow, with a lot of help. But there were days I thought I wasn't going to. Now that I have, I want to give something back."

I asked him about movies like *Boyz 'n the Hood*. They approached the unfortunate truth, he admitted, although he had some doubts about the stereotypes that resulted from it. His main concern was the lack of context in drawing these pictures of Black youth: where do the drugs come from? Who sells them? Why are the neighbourhoods run down? Where are the opportunities? In his soft drawl, Danny told me the hard truth: there is still racism in America. The racism comes not just from White Americans but also from other minorities like Jews and Asians. "They made it. Why can't we?

That's their attitude. They don't want to see the differences between us and them. They just think we grumble too much. If you're young in America, there are a lot of problems. If you're young and Black, like I said, chances are you're just trying to survive."

President Clinton was encouraging young Americans like Danny to actively help with social problems. The plan was for an optional form of national service, for youth to work with other youths at the grassroots. It would try to replicate and spread successful programmes that cities like Boston have run. But that may not be enough. The problems of youth in today's America are considerable. In 1990 alone, some 3,000 teens were murdered and 2,200 killed themselves. Every day, an average of 2,000 drop out of school. Youth unemployment is 19 per cent, and over 14 million kids live below the poverty line. Drugs are an increasing problem, perhaps the number-one cause of youth going to prison.

More than this, America's youth are under attack – not by rival gangs or drug pushers – but by their elders. "Who are our children?" the Los Angeles Times asked. "One day, they are innocent. The next, they may try to blow your heads off." Many adults reacted to the troubled youth of America not with empathy and help, but out of fear and a desire for retaliation. Some legislation allowed teenagers to be tried as adults, rather than in family courts, so tougher sentences could be imposed. In New York City alone, 28 kids between 13 and 15 were indicted for murder in 1993. They could then be put into jail with older, hardened criminals or might even be eligible for the death penalty, if that is re-instituted. In schools, metal detectors sought out those who came to class with guns and knives in their lunchboxes. In over 1,000 places across America, from Newark and Phoenix to small towns like Athens in Alabama, curfews required teens to be off the street by midnight. Many of Generation X will not be counselled and coached by their parents. They will be confined to their rooms at night or put in jails, controlled and even criminalised. "The country's war on crime," one report warned, "is fast becoming a war on teenagers."

Some like Danny argue that underlying causes — poverty, the breakdown of the family, lack of education, opportunity and jobs — must be addressed in a coherent youth policy. But such messages seemed lost in the panic for the quick fix of curfews, metal detectors and prisons.

❖

There was a students' house across the street from the ivy-covered law school. It was a place known for its well-stocked bar and wild parties; a watering hole for students from one of America's best universities. Some of them, at least. Minorities like Danny were not present. Women like Anna-Lise, activists and feminists, did not go.

On a Friday night in late spring, the place was crowded, jammed around the bar. The air was warm and sticky-sweet. Rock music blared from speakers hung from corners of the room. The average student here was White and of that species of young Americans known as "party-animals". But among the crowd, there was a young woman who was a teacher. A teacher, moreover, in an inner city school. She talked about the struggle to motivate children who had no role models, no parents to stress academic achievement. She told about a friend who was confronted by a young boy with a gun. She confessed that exhaustion from that teaching life had brought her back to graduate school. After completing her Master's in education, she would decide if she should return to teaching, or look for an easier and better-paying option.

"Don't be a sap," one of the law school students told her. "You hang out with losers, and you're going to be a loser too." He said it, then threw back another beer. There was something casual, almost slick in the way he dispensed his advice. He, like her, was in his mid-20s. He started to tell her about his ambitions. The top few of his class would be able to choose from an array of jobs that paid $100,000 or more; he was going to be one of them.

He rattled on. She stirred her drink. Then she turned away from him. Later, she said she was so mad with his attitude that she wanted to tell him off.

"Why didn't you?" I asked.

"Part of me wanted to," she said, weary. "Another part of me thought he might just be right."

REBUILDING COMMUNITY The professor stood next to the fireplace and stared straight ahead. "Social credit is the answer," he said, rubbing his chin and distinguished growth of hair. "We need institutions that build our sense of society and community. Like our churches and associations used to."

It was a talk in Cabot House, one of the university's grand undergrad houses. The room had windows that overlooked the river. The lights were dim. We sat on comfy old armchairs. Around the empty fireplace, we listened to the professor. He drew on anecdotes about different states in Italy where he did his research and about which he had now written a book. After re-telling the history of Italian towns from medieval times, the professor turned coy. What factor was the most consistent co-relation to good government — was it education, wealth? He did not give the answer straightaway but asked the students to guess. He shook his learned head at one suggested answer after another; his smile was almost a smirk. He frowned at me when my guess was civil society — meaning voluntary groups like parents' associations and neighbourhood committees. Then his smile returned as someone again guessed "education".

His conclusion after many years of work and analysis was that governments work best where there are choral singing groups. Not that democracy and good government responded to sweet voices; rather, that the choral singing group was a common voluntary association in Italy, alongside amateur football clubs. Voluntary associations were the recurring feature in states that did better; far more so than wealth or education levels. The professor then went on to call for institutions that could create "social credit". If the country could foster more occasions for citizens and neighbours to come to work together and know each other, he believed that American democracy would strengthen, that problems of crime and social tension would lessen.

During the discussion that followed his talk, we met. The professor suggested that I came close to guessing his answer because I had read his book. I had not even heard about his recently-released book until he mentioned it, and told him so. I tried to tell him that civil society has been a concern for those in Asia who were thinking about how democracies function. I also tried to give credit where it was due: that the history of early America, since the first pilgrim settlers to the groups that headed West, was one of voluntary associations; a point strongly argued by the historian Daniel Boorstein in his book *The Americans*. The professor smiled blandly and turned to someone who had a question about Italy and his work there. "Community," he said, rubbing his beard, "is what we need."

Americans, like the professor and Amitai Etzioni, a lecturer in a Washington DC university, have been putting forward "communitarian" ideas. Compared to the traditional liberal emphasis on freedom and the individual and the role of government, these communitarians stress civic responsibilities, groups and self-help. Such ideas have won a hearing among some politicians but lack widespread appeal. Some liberals are simply illiberal about new and contrary ideas. Others complain that the proposals of communitarians – like doing jury service, serving on the board of a neighbour-hood school – do not go far enough. That criticism may be right, given that America's neighbourhoods have become so widely differentiated, between affluent sub-urbs and troubled inner-city areas, between safe and crime-prone neighbourhoods, between have and have-nots. What about communities that are so poor or divided by crime and violence that they cannot participate in self-help groups? Who will contribute time to these voluntary associations? Is the professor suggesting that women must stay home in order to volunteer time for church and other organisations?

The debate went on into the evening, like so many college-room discussions did. There were clever questions from the audience, mainly young undergrads. There were elegantly framed comments and retorts by the professor. There were a few witticisms. But always, it seemed, there were more questions than answers.

A few days later, I was talking to Linus and Karen. We were trying to fix a date to meet for dinner. But the Wednesday we had in mind was impossible. They had a PTA meeting; a meeting of the Parents and Teachers Association of the school their children attended, a Montessori school.

The school was a private institution, funded mainly by the parents, who had a big share in deciding on how the school should try to educate their children. I had visited the school, a low building in a quiet neighbourhood, some two or three blocks from where we lived. It was next to a city park, a large one with bicycle paths, jungle gym sets for the children, football and baseball fields, picnic tables and even a small area of wet marsh where wading birds could be spotted. It was a good setting for the school which believed that children learnt best through play rather than compulsion. It was a safe place. In the streets nearby, there were conspicuous yellow signs to warn motorists that there was a school for children in the vicinity and they must drive with caution. There was little crime or drugs. The building itself seemed designed specially as a school for younger children, with splashes of colour that attracted your eye as you entered.

The air was noisy with the children's voices but not rowdy. The teacher seemed to have things under control even if there was no fixed state syllabus that the school must follow. The classes were small enough to allow interaction with the teacher. The Koh kids enjoyed it, and their parents seemed satisfied at their progress. There seemed to be few of the problems that were associated with schooling in America.

"That's because it's not a state school," Linus said. "If you go to a government-funded school, you have to go to the one in your neighbourhood. Now, if you're in a good area, that may be okay. But if you're in a poor area, forget it. Schools get some funding from both state and federal government but the crucial difference is how much support the surrounding community can give it. They raise money for schools with local property taxes. So if the neighbourhood is rich, with high-value properties and owners who can pay, the schools have more resources. We weren't sure about the schools in Central Square, so we chose the Montessori school. But the fees for the three kids are almost as much as one year's tuition at Harvard! The good thing is that the school allows the parents a big say in how things are run. At the PTA meeting we're going to decide on what the kids should be doing, what direction their education is going to take. The teachers have their ideas but the one thing that is great here is they will also take your suggestions. They feel that educating the children is something that the parents and the community as a whole must have a strong hand in."

Some time later, at a picnic the Kohs organised in the park near the school for their son's birthday, I got to meet some of the other parents in this community. PTAs are, I had learnt by this time, one of the most active community groups in America, although the level of participation seems to be tailing off, rather than increasing. I thought back to the professor's talk about community in America, when the parents began to arrive. There was a Chinese opera singer and his wife who had come to America to seek fame. There was an Australian who designed furniture. There was someone from Louisiana, and two who grew up in small, New England towns before coming to Cambridge for university and then work. Others with children at the school included Harvard professors, local politicians, engineers and other professionals. They were all able to afford the education at the school but, in other respects, they were a diverse bunch.

The children played. The parents looked on, nibbling at the food the Kohs had provided and chatting among themselves, talking mainly about the children. However, they were never so preoccupied that they could not break off mid-sentence to make sure a child would not wander off or begin a fight, and that they would have enough to eat and drink. They talked about the education system, its weaknesses in America as a whole. They exchanged some horror stories about schools in other neighbourhoods. The government was doing a terrible job, they seemed to agree, especially in the poor areas. They then shared their hopes about what they could do through the PTA to make things better for their children. I listened. I wanted to ask how, without similar resources of time and money, others who were poorer could hope for the same, good education. But, without my own child, a stake in the school, I was not part of their community or any other.

the gunshot of
freedom

AMERICAN public discussion is a bag of potato chips passed around in the middle of an entertaining show. TV forums snap, crunch and provide crisp sound-bites but they are – like chips – largely short of substance and real food for thought. The debate on the North American Free Trade Agreement, or NAFTA, was flavoured accordingly. Even the debate in the Senate and Congress, televised 24 hours a day on C-Span, was a succession of punchy lines; a buffet of political snack food. This despite the recognition that NAFTA meant much more than trade of goods and services. That it was a collision of different strands in the American character: the robust, expansionist against an individualistic, even isolationist, creed.

In the weeks and months before the Congress vote, an unusual coalition formed against the issue. To them, NAFTA was about jobs, the threat that American jobs would head south to cheaper Mexican labour. It was about America being unable to enforce environmental and labour standards against Mexican products. To some, it meant partnership with a government in Mexico City that they considered undemocratic. For these and other reasons, labour unions, consumer groups and advocates like Ralph Nader, fringe environmental groups and many radical intellectuals came together against NAFTA. Even the Democratic leader in Congress, Richard Gephardt, spoke out against it. But the man spearheading the effort in the media was Ross Perot, the small and feisty Texan billionaire turned politician. After a strong showing as a third candidate in the 1992 presidential election, Perot seemed to pick this issue as one on which he could again make an impact and establish himself as a credible force, outside traditional Democratic and Republican parties.

Clinton had staked his presidency on the effort. His team worked on bi-partisan lines with pro-business Republicans. They dragged out the former presidents, including the still popular Ronald Reagan, former secretaries of state and of the treasury to endorse the policy. The rare businessmen whom the public liked, like Lee Iacocca, the man who saved Chrysler, also made TV appearances for NAFTA. However, in the sound-bite warfare of TV, the anti-NAFTA coalition always had the advantage. They seemed more like the average American than the suit-wearing NAFTA proponents. They were the ones who were good and mad about the issue, attitudes which some Americans tended to associate with sincerity. Compared to the rational economists and businessmen in favour of NAFTA, they had the better quips: "American jobs are at stake," a workers' representative protested. "Put Americans first." Such slogans were catchy, snack-food for those hungry for a cause. The rejoinder by economists and businessmen – that in a borderless economy, low-wage jobs will always go elsewhere – proved harder to digest, even if it might have been true.

It was against this background that I visited Congress in Washington DC on the day of the last debate, just before the vote. Outside the famous Capitol building with its stately dome, the issue came alive. Groups stood on the broad grey steps, chanting out their slogans, waving their placards and banners for and against NAFTA. "Will you approve it with the fraudulent illegal and criminal Mexican government?" one asked. A few feet away, a smaller pro-free trade poster asked for "NAFTA Now!" Policemen were on hand to keep the peace. Words were exchanged and rival posters were displayed, but there seemed to be little threat of violence. Half a dozen camera crews moved around, each with an anchorman or -woman talking into a mike to capture the sound and fury of the moment. I was one among a number who walked among the crowd, not marching, without banners. The groups continued to chant their slogans as I passed.

I fell into a conversation with another on-looker. Susan was a pleasant-faced woman in her early 50s, a teacher in a high school. She was in Washington on an education grant to research better ways of teaching the American Constitution, the foundation stone of the country's democratic system. She knew the city well, having worked in the 1960s on the staff of a congressman. "What do you think?" she asked once she learnt I was a foreigner, waving at the scene around us. I declined comment at first, deferring to her knowledge as both an American citizen and a teacher of its constitution. She meant to encourage me by sharing her own views.

"I'll tell you frankly. I love it. I love to see people who have organised themselves like this, who can take time out for the bigger issues which concern us all. When I used to work on the Hill, people would call my congressman all the time – complete strangers from his district – and they would expect to be put through to him so they could tell him what they thought. When I think of that, I believe our democracy's working. It's in good shape. But I also worry. I've heard that it's special interests and lobby groups from industry who have the most influence. That's the kind of groups that get the congressman's ear, not real people. I think if we can find some way to make sure everyone gets access, things would be better."

What did she think of America's social problems? "Well, I really saw things differently once I left DC. Or rather when I stopped working on the Hill. There's something called the Beltway mentality. It takes its name from the highway that circles DC, the Beltway. For some, the rest of America might as well not be there. Nothing is important if it doesn't happen here in DC, and we can do anything so long as it doesn't affect DC. That's why I think it's so important that people outside DC and politics, ordinary Americans, can get their message through. So what do you think?"

I wondered how, if Washington did not consider things beyond the Beltway, it could understand events across the Pacific, half a world away. But I did not say that. I found her faith in the ordinary American admirable. I told her of some Asian societies which experienced a quieter politics, in which the citizen may have less influence beyond the vote. "Things will change," she replied with a sympathetic smile, speaking slightly louder so I could hear her above the protest chants. It did not occur to her that some may prefer their politics quieter.

With Susan's enthusiasm and help, I obtained a pass to enter the Congress that the anti- and pro-NAFTA factions were trying to influence. The House was less than half full. Congressmen and women were debating, or rather making their speeches. No one seemed to speak more than a few minutes, but everyone had to have their say. Most had made up their minds and had their speeches prepared and typed up. Others, still undecided, were not there. They were meeting in the corridors of power or in White House rooms where President Clinton and staff waged their mini-campaign to push through NAFTA.

The anti-NAFTA lobby looked like winning at the start. Even if they thought it was correct, congressmen were running away from NAFTA, from the possibility of doing something unpopular that might cost them votes at the next election. When someone sought to change their minds, it was more than principles that were used. Many congressmen held out on their vote until special government projects and expenditure were promised for their districts, to boost the local economy and, thereby, their popularity. That was what helped the pro-NAFTA lobby make a late, and finally successful, surge. President Clinton talked about NAFTA as America's future. But the politics surrounding this monumental political decision was unsettlingly mixed up with old-fashioned pork barrel persuasion.

While the pro-NAFTA forces finally won, what intrigued me was the strength of their opponents. Seeing America from abroad, the image is expansive. The country is involved in everything from security to trade, art and industrial investment, to the point that some speak of America as empire, imperialist. The American tendency to isolationism seemed a thing of the past, factors in WW I and WW II which the wars themselves had made redundant. The NAFTA debate was the view from the inside. It highlighted that isolationist strand of the American political character was still real and strong. It revealed that many Americans had little appetite for world trade and interconnections. Bred on individualism, self-reliance and a measure of isolation, they believed that they got along best without the rest of the world. Put Americans first, buy American: it was more than a statement about economics.

❖

Going to a lake set among the woods in early fall may seem a fine escape from the rattle of such slogans. But, in this case, it brought me to one source of their rhetoric – a small lake in the northeast of the country, some 20 minutes drive from where we lived – Walden Pond. If

America values the individual and isolation, its first poet and philosopher must be Henry David Thoreau, and its spiritual text *Walden*. In 1846, Thoreau lived out his principles of self-sufficiency. He lived on the shores of this lake for one year, in a small, rough cabin he made with his own hands, alone, away from the prosperous town and people of nearby Concord. *Walden*, his book of that experience, extolled individualism. "If a man does not keep pace with his companions, perhaps it is because he hears a different drummer," Thoreau wrote. "Let him step to the music he hears, however measured or far away." I was a teenager when I first read those words. In the adolescent angst of those years, such sentiments were a wisdom – as they have been to innumerable teenagers in the 150-or-so years since publication. *Walden* has endured as an American classic.

Thoreau's cabin has stood the test of time less well. Only its foundation stones remain. A historical society has placed pillars and chains to show where it stood. Imagination must supply the rest. Next to the site, there is a pile of rocks. Each visitor, by tradition, places one to mark a visit. What would the hermit-poet have made of NAFTA? "We are in a great haste to construct a magnetic telegraph from Maine to Texas," Thoreau commented on one of the projects of his day. "But Maine and Texas, it may be, have nothing important to communicate." Extend the analogy just across the border from Texas to Mexico, change the technology from telegraph to satellite links and trade and – across the gap of years – there is Thoreau's isolationist answer, emphasising self-sufficiency.

But that should not be taken as the only response in America. Countervailing values exist, not only in the contemporary world but even from Thoreau's time. New England in the mid-19th century, when Thoreau lived in his cabin, was not a hermit kingdom but a hub of industry and trade. And one of the most popular, if unlikely, commodities of the region was ice.

Making the best of severe winters, in the days before the modern refrigerator, a man named Frederic Tudor began exporting ice. He developed better ways of cutting and storing it for shipping. He stimulated consumer demand by making ice-drinks and ice-cream fashionable. Tudor began selling beyond the warmer regions of the US and expanded overseas. By 1846, some 65,000 tones were shipped to faraway destinations such as the Caribbean, South America, China, the Philippines, Australia, India and Singapore. In Singapore, nearly 150 years ago, businessman and pioneer Whampoa Hoo Ah Kay imported Tudor's New England ice. He stored it in his then-famous ice-house on Clarke Quay.

One of the sources of Tudor's ice was Walden Pond. Thoreau sat there, watching over 100 men in Tudor's employ carry out the ice-harvesting of the lake. He mused how "the pure Walden water is mingled with the sacred Ganges". He did not talk about world trade. At lakeside in the summer, it is hard to hear the hermit-philosopher's voice. The water is cool and clear. But the sandy beach near the cabin is crowded with sunbathers and swimmers. The narrow paths by the edge of the water are eroded by the footfall of too many visitors. Their hiking and sports shoes, although branded as Nike,

Reebok or something else, are made in Asia. The carpark is crammed with cars. Most of them are made in Japan or, even if in Detroit, have significant foreign components.

Today, in the late 20th century, America may need more Tudors than Thoreaux. But perhaps it always has. Thoreau's neighbours in Concord deplored the poor-quality clothes the poet made and patched in the name of self-sufficiency. They considered his cabin an eye-sore. Once he moved out, his neighbours dismantled it to re-use piecemeal in fixing their barns. Thoreau was an uncommon champion of the human spirit free of social constraints but the daily trade of life was based on commoner sense. It is Thoreau's thinking about the human spirit, rather than his economics, that lives on. In politics, in social relations, the American as individual is an enduring myth. The individual that has rights and is empowered to achieve his or her full potential, to seek happiness. It is this that is Thoreau's contribution to the American dream.

Those ideas, Thoreau's elegant words and example, had brought me, ironically, from much further away than Texas or Mexico, to retrace the journey of Tudor's ice backwards from Singapore to Walden. I searched along the ground and under a bright sky for a rock. Then I placed it on the pile beside Thoreau's cabin.

❖

After Clinton's victory over NAFTA, a number of political observers believed that a corner had been turned in his presidency. They became believers in the administration that had started off with difficulty, controversially, by moving to allow gays in the military. Success in NAFTA, they suggested, was the beginning of a recovery for a president whose public image had suffered from a Beverly Hills haircut as much as ineffectual policies on places from Bosnia to Somalia. The months that followed showed such optimism was misplaced.

The president flip-flopped over China's record on human rights, blinking when they stared him down by refusing to put up token reforms to secure the renewal of their "most favoured nation" trading status, known in headlines as MFN. Clinton, the candidate who criticised then incumbent Bush about being soft on China, became the president who instead de-linked human rights and the MFN. The health care reform, a central pledge in Clinton's campaign, turned terminal, suffocated by the voluminous report put in by First Lady Hillary and her advisors. Even on the issue of crime, where there was so much public demand for government to get tough, the Crime Bill remained dead-locked in Congress until last-minute campaign-style persuasion squeaked it by.

Through it all, Clinton's standing in the all-important polls of public opinion and approval sank. By the time mid-term elections came around, the president's party seemed in disarray. Democratic favourites were unseated, including New York State governor Mario Cuomo, a man many felt could have been president. Clinton and the politics he stood for seemed unsupported, vulnerable. To be endorsed by the president in 1994 was a liability. Everyone took potshots at him. Most literally, one citizen drove to the White House in a pick-up truck and fired his rifle, knocking out a window. Less literally, American voters turned the mid-term election of Congress and Senate into a landslide for Republicans. The rifleman was stopped and disarmed by on-lookers. No one was quite sure what to do about the voters and critics.

The American attitude to their leaders is very different from practices in some Asian countries, where "respect" may seem to some to border on subservience. They take it as part of their freedom of speech. More than that, many Americans believe that it shows the strength of their democracy. A criticism, a joke, sniping: all can be endured without the system failing.

❖

Our favourite place to eat in Boston sat on a busy street where cars were always double-parked. The block was low and old, opposite a late-night liquor store. Further up the street, there was an Irish bar, a Salvation Army thrift shop, and a second-hand book and record store attended by an Asian woman who hardly spoke any English.

The Vietnamese restaurant, "Pho Pasteur", seemed to fit in there. It dished up bowls of hot, tasty noodles and plates of crispy spring rolls, as well as more elaborate dishes like pigeon. The flavours were an imperfect reminder of home for us: not Singaporean, but still Asian. Others too were attracted; the clientele seemed more or less equally divided between White and Asian. Over the year, the restaurant expanded into the vacant shop next door, doubling its size, and was still full for lunch and dinner. Another Asian immigrant made good in America.

To get to Pho Pasteur, we drove along the perimeter between two districts of the city: Allston and Brookline. The restaurant was in Allston, in a more or less typical block. Madge, another Singaporean, lived within walking distance of it. Some nights she reported hearing gunfire in the streets.

Brookline was a different place. There was good shopping, a cinema centre that showed art films and, further out, a chic mall with Bloomingdale's, the up-market department store. A number of hospitals and clinics were also situated in the area, some of them world leaders in medical treatment.

When driving to the restaurant, I avoided going past the hospitals although sometimes, unaccustomed to the routes, we went that way. On those occasions, we witnessed crowds outside the clinics, protesting against abortions. No one fought or threw fire bombs. No bricks were thrown. There was little sense of pandemonium or fear. The protest was with words, spoken and on placards. The protesters crowded the sidewalk. The ugliness came when doctors or a woman headed into one of the clinics. Then the protesters would stand in the way, calling out "baby killer" or some other slur. The police were often present but unless the protesters physically obstructed those trying to get into the clinic, they did not interfere. Verbal intimidation is an exercise of the freedom of speech.

Our friend Danna went down to the area to work now and again, as part of her rotation between different hospitals. She told us of her experience as a doctor and a woman. "It's terrible, I tell you. They yell right at you. Some even spit at you. I mean, abortion is legal and we're just doing our job. And yet it goes on all the time. You know what really gets me? It's when I look at the protesters. Most of them are men. Middle-aged, White men. What right do they have to make a woman's choice? I mean, the women I meet don't go for abortions lightly. It's a difficult decision as it is. Let alone to have to go through this gauntlet that the protesters create. By the time they get into the clinic, some of the women are crying. Just crying. The irony is that all the women who go in are treated that way, even if they have no intention to have an abortion, even if they just have an appointment for an ultra-sound scan."

For years, the abortion debate has raged across the country. There is no sign of compromise between the so-called "pro-life" movement and the "pro-choice" factions. The divisions have, instead, become sharper. These politics focused to make it necessary for any electoral candidate to have a position on abortion and the language became increasingly incendiary. Besides Danna, I met few people who were against allowing the protests in front of the clinic. It's just words, these people seemed to say. There are no bricks thrown, no violence. Just noise, a bit of a traffic jam. And you don't have to go there; there are other routes around the city. To most, those inconveniences had to be allowed in the name of free speech.

❖

I stood in a field at 5.30 in the morning, waiting for the birth of America. A motley group of men came out of a tavern, with muskets and a look of apprehension beneath their tri-cornered 18th century hats. Paul Revere, having delivered his message that the British were coming, rode off into history on a white horse. The drums of the troops were heard, marching up to confront the militia. Soon, redcoats and revolutionaries would have their first armed clash. Here in this field, in 1775, the American revolution began. From the small town of Lexington came, in Emerson's grandiloquent words, "the shot that was heard around the world".

What I witnessed was re-enactment. Every year, the residents of Lexington and nearby Concord don their costumes to play out this scene. And, despite the early hour, it draws a good crowd. That morning, some 600 people ringed the field in rows of two or three deep. Young boys and girls stole to the front to get a better view, or stood on top of ladders they brought from home. Women drank steaming mugs of coffee and cheered, while their husbands videotaped America's rebirth.

My friend Don Snodgrass was a history buff. Earlier in the year, he and Ann had taken us along what they called the "Battle Road", the route British troops took in marching up to Lexington and Concord for the first confrontation. It was a winding, narrow road, set among wooded park lands and close to a small river. A pleasant drive in Don's tidy Japanese car. On that trip and, again, on the morning that we waited at Lexington's common, Don told me that those who led this confrontation had not known they were starting a full-scale revolution. "At first, they were just tired of being ordered around by the British. The idea of freedom came later," Don said. "Protesters and troublemakers like Samuel Adams are now known as patriots," he added.

There was a distraction during the re-enactment that morning. A short line of people was marching, not in period costume or to watch the event. They carried placards. "Remember Waco", one sign read, referring to the Texas incident in which police stormed the Branch Davidian religious sect, resulting in mayhem and death. The demonstration seemed out of place in such a patriotic setting. On this occasion America should be praised, not protested against. But Don just shrugged. The re-enactment carried on. "It's a free country," someone said quietly.

Freedom is an American icon. Brandeis, the well-known Supreme Court justice, once explained that, "Those who won our independence believed . . . that freedom to think as you will and speak as you think are means indispensable to the discovery and spread of political truth." It is more than a legal proposition. Freedom in America is lived out every day. It is an ideal everyday people hold on to. Consequently, demonstrators are allowed, whether they protest for Waco or against abortions. In part, the experience of revolution suggests that to be an American patriot is to be a protester, a trouble-maker. Similarly, the press in America can report on everything politicians do wrong, from work to mistresses and shady deals. And, beyond press and politics, freedom is expected in daily life. From the type of bread in their sandwich to whether or not the tuna filling is dolphin-free, from hairstyle to lifestyle: Americans assert choice in everything. In the event of a crippling injury, they even want the choice to be sustained by a machine or to turn it off. As car licence plates in New Hampshire proclaim, "Live Free or Die."

The world is now more complicated than America's founding fathers had imagined, as are the potential problems of freedom. So while it is still highly valued, it would be wrong to think freedom is completely unfettered in America. Protest marches can be limited according to time, place and manner, although they will not be stopped outright. If someone incites violence, the police can step in. Under President Clinton, laws of this nature were introduced in respect of anti-abortion protests, to ensure that people have access to the clinics. *Playboy* magazine is not banned by the government but, in many towns, public pressure by conservative groups keeps it out of supermarkets, or discreetly hidden on the magazine rack. If the press is motivated by malice in their reporting of a public figure, they can be sued, but not if they were simply wrong in fact.

In America, like any other country, there are limits and standards. The difference is a question of degree, the way limits to freedom are accepted or challenged.

Driving provides a good, everyday analogy. In many countries, you can only make a U-turn where there is a sign allowing it. In America, it is the reverse: on ordinary roads, you can do it unless there is a sign saying you cannot. The individual American, every single one of them, is given the autonomy to decide when and where to make that turn. Freedom is the assumption. Such freedom can of course be abused. To leave matters of taste and style largely to the individual, the law at an extreme upholds near-obscene words or the burning of the American flag on the basis that "one man's vulgarity is another's lyric".

But sometimes it seems to work. The free American press exposed the unethical dirty tricks of Watergate, bringing down President Nixon. People can say what they think, whether in important forums or everyday conversation, without worrying about government censorship. That morning in Lexington during the re-enactment of America's first struggle for freedom, the Waco protesters exercised their freedom to protest while others exercised the freedom to ignore them. Nothing got out of hand between the two groups.

That is the promise that comes with words of protest and freedom in America. And then, on the way home after the re-enactment of America's birth and freedom, I got a little lost and made a U-turn, even when no sign said I could.

❖

Some months later, on a cold and grey day, Jin Hua and I went again to our favourite Vietnamese restaurant in Allston for a bowl of noodles and hot soup. The traffic was slow on the wet roads but I took the shorter route, avoiding the cluster of hospitals in Brookline and the obstruction of protesters. We enjoyed our lunch and then ran other errands. I only heard it on the evening news, although we had been just a short distance from it all.

A man came out of the usual crowd of protesters. Stepping into the Planned Parenthood clinic, he pulled out a rifle from a duffle bag and began shooting. Then he slipped the weapon under his arm and calmly went out, back onto the street. He headed for another abortion clinic, Preterm, along Beacon Street. Again the rifle fired. Two victims died. Both of them women. Both of them employees at the clinics, not clients seeking abortions. Seven others were hospitalised with gunshot wounds. The gunshot spoke for those who called themselves "pro-life". The protest had gone beyond words.

That night a candlelight vigil was organised. Quickly, President Clinton and state politicians condemned the violence. "Moral questions," Massachusetts Governor William Weld said, "cannot be answered by violence." Some within the pro-life or anti-abortion movement also spoke out against the violence. But outside the clinics where the murders took place, others continued to yell anti-abortion slogans. Neither police nor a sense of decency prevented them.

The Brookline shootings were not an isolated incident. In 1993, guns, not words, had provided the anti-abortion argument in four instances; twice in Pensacola, Florida. But the geography of the incident at hand, its location on the streets I knew and had walked or driven by, made it more real than any headline. I could no longer remember the protests as just a nuisance. And still later, after I had returned to Singapore, I was not able to remember the Waco protesters I had seen that morning in Lexington with innocence. A government building in Oklahoma City was devastated by a bomb. The reason for the bombing was said to have been the Waco incident. I wondered if any of the protesters I had seen that early cold morning in Lexington had been involved, if the words of protest had not been twisted to legitimise violence. That is the danger that comes from words and freedom in America; the gunshot of freedom.

the politics of
belonging

"To say of someone that 'he is of American stock' has come to mean that he is white, probably Protestant and of Anglo-Saxon descent, and that his forebears emigrated to America some generations back."

Max Lerner, *America as a Civilization*

SOCCER AND BEING A MINORITY We know who won the 1994 World Cup, the first to be held in the United States. It is less certain, however, if the World Cup won America. The country loves sports. Star players become household names, celebrities, role models and millionaires. American sports fans compare rushing yards of Emmitt Smith to Thurman Thomas, debate whether the present-day Knicks are better than the last championship team and collect baseball cards. Heroes like Michael Jordan and Joe Montana form part of modern-day folklore; everyone knows their strengths and deeds. Sports, it is said, is one subject you can talk to anyone about. "Did you see the game?" is a gambit that starts conversation throughout the country. From the new employee to his CEO, from factory workers to professors, sports provides common ground.

The place of soccer in all this is, however, uncertain. It is basketball, American football and baseball – the Big Three – that dominate this modern-day pantheon of gods. They hog the headlines in the newspaper sports sections and prime-time coverage on ESPN, the sports channel. Other games get attention only occasionally, perhaps when the Olympics, US Open, US Masters or Indianapolis 500 are on. Normally, they are buried on page 80 or worse – unless someone achieves notoriety, like ice-skater Tonya Harding who conspired to injure rival Nancy Kerrigan. On the common ground of American sports, the Big Three stand at the very centre. Soccer is an outsider.

No one cares that two of the Big Three are almost unknown outside this continent; that few people outside America know who almighty Emmitt Smith is, let alone the lesser players in the country's parochial sports. Conversely, no American can comprehend that the rest of the world loves soccer. This remains the case despite a successful 1994 World Cup with record attendances, good TV ratings, record-level sponsorship, a $25-million surplus, low violence, healthy spin-offs for hotels and – by the way – its share of interesting games. Many American sports journalists still crinkle their noses at soccer. They complain about the lack of goals, statistics and commercial breaks. Most tellingly, some call soccer a "silly foreign game".

Surveys in the US show that children and women like soccer, as do first-generation immigrants in America's melting pot; not the stereotypical American sports spectator with his TV, EZ chair lounger and six-pack of beer. The World Cup, and a good showing by Team USA, helped. But soccer still raises questions about what is and is not American. It threatens to incorporate the country into a world system in which non-Americans are the heroes and Brazil, not this country, is number one. The gut reaction of many American sports fans is therefore to defend the primacy of the Big Three. The flag-waving ideal in this country is not soccer, but basketball's "Dream Team" at the last Olympics that united the country's best-known and best-paid professionals to thrash all other countries. The next test of American willingness to join in the world's most popular sport will come with Major League Soccer, which started in 1995 with twelve professional American teams. A previous attempt had died a decade ago.

To do better, soccer must face up to a common xenophobia and become all-American. Pizza, originally from Italy, and German hot dogs and hamburgers once made that transition. They are now as ubiquitous and as loved as Mum's apple pie. Like a new immigrant, soccer must work hard, learn to speak American and buy a TV (or, in this case, be on TV). If so, it would soon fit in, slip into the mainstream, become all-American.

Other imports are more resistant to inclusion. Unlike many European immigrants – Irish, Italian, Polish,

Jewish – other races do not blend in so easily. The first of these that come to mind are the African-American Blacks or Negroes who were brought forcibly to the American continent as slaves. But in today's America, there are also Hispanics or Latinos who have come from Mexico, Central and South America and the Caribbean, most as migrant labour and quite a number, illegally; and Asian-Americans who have crossed the Pacific, as long ago as the 18th century, but also more recently after the Korean and Vietnamese wars, as well as those fresh off the boats, and often illegals.

All across the country, in each of these ethnic groups, there are signs of a growing dissatisfaction with the idea of integration, of giving up their separate cultural identities to enter the mainstream of a predominately White and male America. Those who favour this speak of an assertion of identity and multi-culturalism that will add variety and validity to the existing social structures, not simply accept them. Multi-culturalism, they urge, will strengthen the country. Others, like the eminent historian Arthur Schlesinger, worry about what he has called the "disuniting of America".

Good or bad, "multi-culturalism" or "disuniting", the phenomenon is palpable on America's campuses. All universities go out of their way to assure applicants that there is no racial prejudice in admissions. To convert that policy into reality, the administrators then make every attempt to recruit good "minority" candidates. Although no quotas are set solely on the grounds of ethnicity, there is a lingering suspicion that the scholastic requirements for minorities is lower than those for

White candidates. Other problems exist with the composition of the staff. At Harvard, shortly before I got there, one of the few African-American professors at the law school took no-pay leave to protest against the lack of any female Black professors on the staff. After a while, his protest led to him being sacked.

Among the students on campus, each ethnic minority group had its separate associations, clubs and activities. Less formal ethnic cliques could also be observed in canteens and within study groups. Racially mixed groups were seen but formed the exception rather than the norm. Some, like Michelle, an African-American girl I got to know, felt social pressure. Not only to be part of the group, but also to avoid too much interaction with others outside the group.

"It was like that in school too," she told me. "I went to a mixed high school. My grades were good, and I mixed with White kids as well as Black. After a while, I noticed my Black friends, some I'd known for a very long time, were avoiding me. It took some time to learn why. When one of them told me, I was shocked. It wasn't just that they wanted me to spend less time with the White students. It was that they somehow thought that doing well in school was a 'White' thing. When they said that, I knew there was something wrong."

One day in late spring, someone tried to organise a "rainbow coalition" day rally at the university. They hoped to bring together students from the different ethnic groups to display the strength of multi-culturalism. Other minority groups were also invited: feminists, gays. But less than forty students turned up, which included the organisers of the event – or, as Americans would remark, the "non-event". The failure was stark, given that most events organised by one particular ethnic group were much better supported. "People aren't into cooperation and rainbow coalitions," Michelle explained. "They each have their own club, their own agendas."

Somewhere in the development of ethnic consciousness, a seemingly natural and not unhealthy urge to be with those of similar background has become a less welcome policy. Multi-culturalism of this sort does not bring people of different races together; rather it excludes others of a different ethnicity. What results is almost a self-created, segregated ghetto; as Michelle said, "Each has their own club." Schlesinger criticises this aspect of multi-culturalism. As he and others see it, the civil rights movement in the 1960s wanted integration. The landmark legal decision, *Brown v. The Board of Education*, struck out against segregated schools and the idea of a separate but equal treatment of races. "Include us" was the main cry. The present trend, however, is quite the opposite of what the civil rights movement wanted for the Black American. "On our own" seems the new emphasis.

It is a change that affects politics at every level of society. It can also be felt at a personal level. One day I was walking through Langdell Hall in the law school with an African-American classmate. We were talking when he met another African-American student. Our conversation stopped. I was not introduced. He turned his attention wholly to the newcomer. His manner of speaking changed too, from his slight drawl to something harder, more street-wise. Then the encounter was over and his language changed back. We carried on with our conversation but it was not the same as before. There is a circle within which some belong and some don't. The circle, moreover, is not always drawn on similar interests or points of view but almost wholly on ethnic differences.

Some African-Americans try very hard to live up to the first part of their self-description, to be more "African". Drew told me that when he first went to college, he felt his ethnic identity so strongly he was ashamed not to be able to speak anything but English. He wanted to enrol in a language course. The language he almost took was Swahili. Last year, he went to Ghana for a study trip, to find the village to which his parents trace their ancestors. It turned out the language there was Yoruba; Swahili, he found out, was an East African language.

The differences did not stop with the question of language. Drew realised that the whole world of cultural difference lay between African-Americans and Africans. "That was where my forefathers came from, you know. That was also the land that people kept telling me was "home". My real home. That's what a lot of Black awareness and literature leads you to believe. But when I got there, I became aware of how much had changed. I was different from them. I was, I am, an American."

Mumbi, a Kenyan classmate, confirmed the other side of the story. "I tried to go to one of their meetings, you know," she said to me in a grumpy, loud voice. "There aren't many Africans here and I thought it would be interesting. I tell you, I didn't fit in at all. They are all so American in their way of thinking. And they couldn't be bothered. It was as if they were looking down at me for coming from Africa. Can you believe it? They say they are so proud of being 'African-American', but they look down on me, an African!

"Those who had visited Africa were the worst. Some of them had the arrogance to believe they could understand Africa from just a two or three weeks' stay. They came to advise us about human rights, about voting, about women's issues: as if they had all the answers. We don't want people from other places to come and tell us what to do. Whether they look Black or not. That's just imperialism all over again. Did you read what they've been saying about female circumcision? They make it sound like all Africans do it, when it's practised by only a small minority. The issue gets completely blown out of proportion. What those women probably need is education, counselling and an alternative way of life. All the outsiders want to do is to hold press conferences."

Her gentle Kikuyu face with its snub features turned gloomy with anger, like a smoking coal. Her heavy-set body, usually easy in its movement, tensed and moved with agitation. Mumbi was a woman who spoke her mind. She had not been happy during her time in America, and that unhappiness cast a shadow over other events.

There was another complaint she made about a feminist discussion group in the law school. The group met once a week or so as a forum for discussion and a self-support group in the predominantly male environment of the law school. After a while, a letter started to circulate. In it, Mumbi and two others – indigenous peoples from Australia, Canada and Africa – complained against their fellow feminists – mainly White Americans, Europeans and Australians. They complained that the White feminists were hogging the forum with "petty" concerns of upper-class liberals. Their concerns – that their peoples are facing poverty and cultural genocide – were excluded. The complaint letter was published in the school's newspaper. It caused consternation in some quarters. There was also guarded laughter among many of the White males. It was a relief to them that, for a change, minorities were not attacking them, but other minorities.

I could not laugh. I was friends with Mumbi and one of the White feminists attacked by the letter. I could imagine that the three feminists who were ethnic minorities may well have felt excluded. But I saw it as a failure on both sides, a failure of the will to cooperate and to belong. I spoke to two of the White feminists. They found it a mystery. They detailed the many ways they had sought to include everyone.

I spoke to Mumbi. She was sure of her exclusion. It seemed inclusion was desired in an America in which everyone claimed a special, minority status whether on ethnic, gender or sexual grounds. Even a minority will have a further minority, whether it is mainstream and ethnic feminists, African-Americans and Africans, Chinese and Vietnamese, established and more recently arrived Hispanics. Such a political fragmentation provides an opportunity for a few within that minority group to rise up and be a leader. King of a smaller realm rather than ordinary citizen. To split off, to declare yourself a minority, or a minority within a minority – as Mumbi and the other ethnic feminists did from the others – is to have power, your own power. Whether Drew and Michelle, or Mumbi and all the others who could point to some difference in race, language, gender or sexual preference, everyone in America is a minority. And no one, it seems, would have it any other way.

NATIVES AND STRANGERS Marchell was a big woman, but comfortable with it and strong. She looked, talked and dressed much like others in the USA. She did not wear feathers or dance with wolves, but she was a Native American from the Patawatomi Pokagon band; what they used to call a "Red Indian". And she was on the warpath. The object of her wrath was mainstream America. For while the Wild West and its cowboys were enduring American myths, regard for the "Red Indian" was less reverent. In old movies, heroes like John Wayne killed them by the hundreds. "Red Indians" – except for Tonto – were blood-thirsty savages with tomahawks who scalped White settlers.

If that was all it was – a celluloid stereotype as out of date as the Keystone cops, as dead as John Wayne himself – things may have been simpler; Marchell, less angry. But another image for "Red Indians", or Native Americans, had arisen, emphasising their spirituality and tradition. Again, the image could be traced to Hollywood, to *Dances with Wolves*. The Kevin Costner movie had popularised this new-age image and, in the process, won awards and made a lot of money. Now, Native

American rituals like sweat-lodges and sacred pipe ceremonies were in fashion. New-age gurus conducted expensive workshops to teach the "Indian way" to non-Indian, mainly White, upper-middle-class professionals.

"It's an improvement," Marchell said of the new-age image. "But it's a very romanticised view. It's almost fashionable to claim you're Native American. I was at a party once and when this girl heard I was Indian, she came up to me. She told me she was one-quarter or one-eighth Indian. I asked her from which tribe and she didn't know. She had grown up White, in a suburb. Now, she wanted to know about her 'roots', all the symbols and rituals. Maybe being White and Christian wasn't colour-ful enough. If that wasn't bad enough, the first thing she asked me was how she could get scholarships for university, as a minority. That's her dream, I guess. Why not? Take all the advantages of being a minority, without any of the pain."

The reality Marchell herself remembered was of growing up in a poor, predominately White area in Indiana. She told her story in a few words. Her face was calm, sometimes allowing an ironic smile. "My father never told me about pipe ceremonies or gods. He wasn't proud of being Indian. It just caused him a lot of pain. There was a lot of prejudice, a lot of misunderstanding. Many of the Indians were uneducated and had no jobs. Many of the men got themselves drunk and were always in or out of trouble. My father's only advice to me was to get a 'White man's education'. We're part German anyway. So I went to school, and I tried to fit in. But I was always made to feel different. The Indian girl.

"One day in school, kids were playing cowboy and red Indians. I watched them play at shooting and killing my people. I also watched the boys who were the red Indians act like blood thirsty savages. After they finished, I spoke about my tribe. 'You can't be an Indian. Your father doesn't wear feathers.' That's what the kids yelled."

Audrey was another Native American, a small girl with washed-out brown hair. She took part in the law school's Shakespearean play and could pass for White if she wanted to. Instead, she had gone out of her way to affirm her ethnicity as a Sioux from Dakota. She spent summers on Indian reservations, to understand her people better. She described a hot and dusty place, with little money and less hope.

"At first they all asked me what I was doing there," she told me. "I mean, I had a choice whether I wanted to go there. They didn't. And they couldn't understand why I had chosen to be with them. At first, they were suspicious. Only after a few weeks, when they saw that I was sincere, did they open up. Only then did I really feel that I belonged. When I was growing up, I knew I was Indian – my mother told me – but I didn't know what that meant. I remember a school visit to a museum. All the exhibits had models of Indians in their traditional costumes. When I told my classmates I was Indian, they refused to believe me. 'All Indians are dead': they said it again and again, refusing to believe me. It was like that old saying, you know. 'The only good Indian is a dead Indian', you heard of that? I guess, to most Americans, that's what we are: good and dead."

We sat next to each other in a class on American constitutional law. When the topic was racial discrimination, her short, fair arm was often in the air, asking for attention. The cases and examples discussed focused on African-Americans and women. Sometimes the teacher referred to Hispanic Americans or even Asian-Americans. But seldom did he mention Native Americans. Audrey interrupted at least once in each class to supply that omission. By the end of the week she was satisfied. "I know a lot of the others may be fed up with me. They just want to get on with the course. But I've got to mention the Native Americans. I just can't sit there and let them ignore us."

Against such a backdrop, the new-age emphasis on Indian spirituality and ceremonies seemed misplaced. Marchell complained, "Sure tradition is important, but 'Indian' ways and dress are important to us like the Pilgrim's dress to modern-day Whites. It's not what we are. This emphasis on our spiritual tradition makes people think only about our past, rather than on the real problems we face now."

Marchell went through the facts and figures with me as we sat in her small and crowded office. A mid-1980s census found that Native Americans had the lowest per capita income of any group in the USA, the highest infant mortality rates and the shortest life-expectancies – only 45 years for men and 48 for women. Indian reservations were often destitute, dusty places far outside the economic mainstream. Opportunities for Native Americans were few. Poverty, alcoholism and drug abuse were endemic. Where reservations had timber or oil, these were exploited by large companies – often with little benefit for the Indians. Sacred sites in Arizona were being used for ski resorts and astronomical observatories. "Indian" mysticism was being taught not by Native Americans but mainly by White new agers.

Marchell was doing some research to stop what she saw as another issue. "American companies use Indian names all the time, like the Jeep Cherokee car, Navajo chips and the Washington Redskins football team. These things have nothing to do with the Indian tribes. They don't get paid for the use of their names. In fact, some legitimise prejudice and stereotypes. Like the Washington Redskins. Can you imagine how African-Americans would react if there was a team called the Washington Darkies?"

"The worst thing about all this discrimination is that the government doesn't even recognise many of the people who are Native Americans. Not just those individuals of mixed blood or who weren't born in a reservation. Whole tribes are waiting to be recognised. They have to go to the court if the government refuses to acknowledge them as Indians. They have to prove lineage. Sometimes, the court even examines if they are living in the "traditional" ways. As if we're still supposed to be living in teepees. It's a difficult process. My own tribe has just been recognised after ten long years of petitioning.

"It's not a formality or a question of what we call ourselves. If you're recognised as an Indian tribe, you get some benefits. It's not a lot considering how much my people have lost, and how much prejudice we face. But if you're not, it's worse. You get the prejudice anyway, and none of the benefits."

I was silent when she finished the litany of problems. There did not seem much to say. It is a far cry for a people who roamed the entire continent before the first White settlers came. Tim Giago, the founder and editor of *Indian Country Today*, wrote that, to some, "The United States is a land with two faces, a land preaching freedom and justice to the world but unable to fulfil those promises to its own indigenous peoples." The Native Americans seemed strangers in their own land, worse off than almost all immigrants, White or otherwise.

The situation explains why Marchell was working at Cultural Survival, a non-profit and non-government body that works on issues facing indigenous people both in the USA and abroad. For when Marchell used the word "we" when she was describing the plight of Native Americans, it was despite the fact that she had graduated from Harvard and then gone on to a law degree. Marchell could have worked in a law firm, passing for White with her part-German ancestry – that would have been the practical thing to do. But, instead, she chose to identify and work for Native Americans. She learnt to say "we" in that natural, easy way of hers. In a similar way, perhaps, she had learnt to analyse the problems facing her people without becoming despondent. "We Native Americans survive," she said with her ironic grin. "Not so many of us now. Not many of us flourishing. But we survive."

There are still some 1.5 million Native Americans in the USA today, Marchell estimated. They are not a powerful community, but there are several Native American congressmen and one senator, Ben Nighthorse Campbell. Although many are not educated, some make it: like Marchell and Audrey. Beyond political representation and education, there is another avenue of influence open to the Native Americans, a somewhat unlikely one: gambling. It is one of the benefits of being recognised as an Indian tribe. Perhaps the most important one.

Until quite recently, US laws were strict on gambling, to which famous Las Vegas and Atlantic City were exceptions. Native Americans, however, have the right to establish casinos on their reservations and to open these to non-Indians – if an agreement can be reached with the state. In 19 states across the country, more than 60 tribes have such agreements. The Indian-run casino in Oneida, Wisconsin started in 1976 as a small-stakes bingo game. By 1994, it employed 1,500 people on a $9 million premises and was estimated to generate some $50 million for the local economy. The Foxwoods Casino in Connecticut, operated by the Mashantucket Pequot Indians, has become the world's largest casino, bringing in about $600 million a year. In all, Native Americans account for $15 billion per year – half of the country's legal gambling industry.

Many Native American leaders believe gambling has worked wonders. Profits have been used to build schools, childcare centres, and transform dusty reservations into boom towns. Many, however, oppose it. Competitors, like tycoon Donald Trump who owns an Atlantic City casino, argues that Native Americans should face the same restrictions as non-Indian developers. Moralists say, without any irony, that Native Americans exploit people.

Some Native American activists see these arguments as ways of keeping them from making money and getting ahead in the modern, money-centred society. They point out that the right to establish reservations, on which gambling can take place, is one of the few rights they were promised in the many treaties by which the White American people took their land. The casinos are, moreover, set up under licensing from the state governments. As such, although controversial, there seems little reason for Native Americans to give up their casinos unless they have another viable economic niche.

I met up with Marchell again after she visited Foxwoods. Her concern was not the casino, but the community centre that was built from the profits. "There were no signs telling you where the community centre was. But the signs for the casino started before you got off the highway. And when you got into town, it was even worse. I drove round and round. I didn't want to go to the casino – I wasn't sure how I'd take it. There wasn't any other choice in the end.

"I stopped at the casino to ask for directions. It was packed, even during the day and in the middle of the week. All White people, mainly people in their 50s or older. There wasn't anything 'Indian' about the casino. The only thing I saw was the uniforms worn by some of the cocktail waitresses. Like squaw dresses, but with high slits to show off their legs. And the waitresses were all White. No one seemed to know where the community centre was. Most didn't even know there was one.

They worked there but all they knew was the casino. Finally, one of the managers knew. He was an Indian. He showed us the way. It was really nice. Very corporate-looking but something to be proud of."

Marchell had gone to visit the Mashantucket Pequot Indians to seek their financial support for a conference to bring Native American leaders from all over the country together. She still was uncertain about the morality of gambling. She wondered what it would do to other Native Americans who did not run casinos and were not rich. Money might splinter the community she had identified with. It might bring into question her own decision to contribute to the cause of Native Americans by study and grassroots action, rather than by setting up blackjack tables and slot machines. But despite these misgivings, Marchell saw something good in the casinos. She believed that the business acumen Indian-run gambling developed and demonstrated allowed them to deal with mainstream society on better terms: "There are things you can do from multi-million dollar offices that you can't from poor reservations."

A STUDENT OF CHINESE Almost every morning from fall to winter, even when the snow was a thick white blanket on the ground, I would wake early and go to the university. In a small building off Bryant Street, near the department of East Asian Civilizations, I would climb two flights of stairs, go through the corridor and enter the classroom as if entering a different world. The teacher, a Mr Bartlett, would come in a few minutes later, and we would greet each other and talk a little. The more we talked, the more I would stumble over my words and he would correct me. In this way, I spent months studying Mandarin at Harvard.

I am not sure why I did it. I had never studied the language before, unlike the majority of Chinese Singaporeans. I was born into a Peranakan family and spoke Malay first, and then English. I went on to study these languages at school and, by the end, my ears were deadened to the inflections of both Mandarin and Chinese dialects. For years, despite all the campaigns in Singapore cajoling us to learn Mandarin as a "mother tongue", I had resisted. It was the lack of time and need. It was also contrarian: the language that my mother had spoken to me, my grandmother and my amah used – my mother tongue, literally – was not Mandarin. I had always maintained I was Singaporean, first and foremost, and did not want to learn Chinese.

I had read many books on the history of China, on Chinese literature and culture as well as books on the diaspora, like Wang Gung Wu's *China and the Overseas Chinese* and Lynn Pan's *Sons of the Yellow Emperor*. As a writer, I had met and talked with many Chinese-language writers, like the well-known Wang Meng from China. These books and experiences had been of great interest but still I did not feel the need for learning the Chinese language. After all, I had accessed these resources in English.

The attempt to begin at Harvard was pragmatic. In contrast to working life, I had more time. The course was free. Meeting White American instructors like Tom Bartlett had, moreover, encouraged me in a way that no teacher who was Chinese could. Bartlett stood, tall and large, with a shock of brown hair, as proof that you did not have to have learnt Chinese from young to speak it. Chinese language and culture, moreover, had never overwhelmed his own core culture; he remained American. Similarly, I was now convinced I could remain Peranakan and Singaporean after learning this new language.

Before I began the course, we met to discuss my reasons and what I hoped to get out of it. His office was in a white house on a quiet street, a former residence turned into a cosy if somewhat crowded department. The room was a little cluttered and small, in relation to Bartlett's size perhaps, but the light came strongly through the window. He explained why people attended his class.

"We're getting many more students now than we did two or three years ago. It's the opening up of the Chinese economy, and all the emphasis on the Pacific. That's the reason for most of our White students. But there's also been a sharp increase in the number of Asian students we get too. Perhaps one-third of most classes are of Asian origin. Korean or even Chinese, but born in America, without a word of Chinese. Of course, they see the practical reasons for Mandarin too.

"But some, quite a few of them I would say, feel that it's part of their identity. They're trying to regain something that they feel is missing after many years of trying to fit into American society. Most of them don't know any Mandarin at all. You don't have to worry about that. If they have had one or two years of learning or can speak basic sentences, we encourage them to go into an accelerated Chinese class. The basic class you'll be attending is for those who hardly know anything to begin with. You should be able to distinguish the pronunciations in the first few classes! You don't have to be embarrassed."

So it was. The White students could not tell the four tones apart. A Korean girl born in California, who had started as a merchant banker before becoming a student of theology, pronounced all the words with an American twang. The Russian student knew the words but sang them out like Jerry Lewis imitating Chinese. In this company, I began with the ultimate encouragement: I was not as bad. Or else, just as bad.

One day, after class, we ended up in a small cake and coffee shop on Massachusetts Avenue, or Mass Ave for short. Adam was teaching Patty, Peter and me Chinese while we ate some brownies with unusually good strong coffee. We had been talking about the rise of China and the implications for the USA. Then the subject had turned to language. Patty and Peter were both from Hong Kong and, with their knowledge of Cantonese, left me behind. But it was Adam who knew more than all of us, who was correcting our pronunciation. It was Adam who had taken Chinese for three years and studied Chinese legal history and archaeology. He was not from Hong Kong. He was White, not Asian. Born in Tennessee, he hoped one day to visit Asia.

Robert was also born in America, in a middle-class neighbourhood in California. Like Adam, he started learning Chinese when he went to university and was fairly proficient. With the skills of law and language, he aimed to get a job in a big New York firm that was keen on expanding into Asia or else to join a university there as an academic. He would fit well into corporate America with his dark, well-groomed hair, his pleasant but ener- getic personality and sharp intelligence. He was one of the upwardly mobile, with his tastes in sushi and his new Golf GTi. Robert, unlike Adam, was Chinese by ethnic- ity, although the difference was not discernible if you closed your eyes when they spoke. They were American in voice, in accent and choice of words, in a way that Peter, Patty or I were not, although we too spoke English. Robert knew this. But he had begun to feel a stronger sense of being Chinese in the past few years.

"You see, where I grew up, my family was the only Chinese family around. The rest of the neighbourhood was all White. Until high school, there was never another Asian in my class. Only when I came to univer- sity did I really mix with other Asians. Then one of my friends took me down to Chinatown. Not just for a meal, but to help out with the tenants' association. That was an eye opener. It was a different world for me: not just the language and the culture, but also the poverty and the concerns with things that I would take for granted. I knew I wasn't one of them. I was born in America, after all. But maybe I also knew I wasn't White."

I learnt more of Asians in America at the prestigious Swarthmore College outside Philadelphia. I had come to give a talk and meet a group of young Asian-Americans. A few of them walked me around the campus, a pleasant place with old buildings of human scale, set amidst trees and flowering shrubs. Afterwards, they hosted a lunch for me to meet a dozen or so of their members. While we talked, I got to know something more of their background. There were a number of Koreans and Japanese whose families had been in America for several generations. They didn't speak any Asian languages. Some had yet to visit Asia. A few others were born abroad, in Taiwan and Vietnam, although they had been in the USA for a decade before going to college. Still others – a Taiwanese and an Indian – had come to America just a few years ago as teenagers. A fair girl of Korean ancestry, with jet-black hair and delicate features, told me about their grouping.

"I know we're all different. I mean, we don't have a country or a language in common. Not even a colour, like South Indians – you know, from India – who are different from those of us from East Asia. Some people don't even think of them when they talk about Asian-Americans. We're not like the Blacks or even the Hispanics. I guess we come together just because we need to.

"The system allows minorities to speak up, but we have to be organised. Take for example what's happening now in Philadelphia. One of the city councilmen spoke out against Asians who were moving their businesses into neighbourhoods that are traditionally Italian. He was an Italian and his message really provoked the community. Last week, a house was burnt down in the Italian quarter. The police say that it was arson, for sure. The house belonged to an Asian family. They all died in the fire. The councilman said that he did not advocate violence. He disclaimed any responsibility. Can you believe that? I can tell you that it was his speech that drove people to this kind of action. So this weekend, a few of us are going down from the college to show our support for a protest that an Asian-American group in the city is organising. That's the only way we can get heard."

That night when I began my talk at the college, I looked up and saw most of the students from the Asian-American group. The majority in the audience were White or African-American, but this group was disproportionately in attendance. They had come in numbers, I suspected, to show their support for me. Perhaps also from an interest in following up on the issues for which we had only a brief time to discuss over lunch. I was, although born in a different place and of a different culture, a fellow Asian. This felt strange and yet also comfortable, comforting. I caught the eye of the Korean girl and, before I started, I retold the audience the story about the Asian family burnt to death in Little Italy, and asked for a minute of silence.

NATION OF IMMIGRANTS Perhaps it was the day. The early summer was cool. The sun and blue skies had already brought out flowers in a profusion of colours and scents. We cycled here along a car-free, carefree path and sprawled on soft grass, picnicking. "Aren't you guys thinking of staying on here?" Ken asked. I looked at Jin Hua. We were puzzled.

Ken was a Chinese Malaysian. He graduated with a PhD and was pursuing state-of-the-art research in molecular biology. He went through secondary school and junior college in Singapore. College education brought him to North America and then, after a stint back in Singapore, graduate studies took him to Miami and then Oregon. Now he worked in a lab that, before it went private, was connected to Harvard University. Married to Danna, an American citizen, he held a Green Card and was on the verge of becoming an American citizen. Once, his situation would have seemed utterly normal. Many people went from Asia to America. Some came as labourers, building much of the railroad, or as refugees, especially from Indo-China. Others were scientists, hi-tech engineers, graduate students who came and never went home; part of the Asian brain drain. From 1960 to 1990, the number of Asians in America increased more than fourfold, from 1.4 to seven million. Asian-owned businesses grew ten times from 1972 to 1985.

But now, when the USA faces economic and social problems and Asia seems in the ascendant, westward migration seems less understandable. Many proclaim the East as the new land of opportunity. Some suggest that old adage, "Go West, young man", be changed in an eastern direction. So why did our friend choose America? And why might anyone think we too would want to stay? At first I thought it was just this one friend. Then, two Singaporeans posed similar questions. Both were pro-fessionals. Bryan had a luxury car, condo and two-child family – all the elements of Singaporean success. Benny had drive, savvy and academic credentials that any corporation would welcome. Even so, both were tempted to stay on here.

"I like the lifestyle," Bryan said. "Americans work hard but they also know how to relax. There's more time for family." He admitted it with a smile. It was a Saturday and his office had closed. We were in our car, headed out to Cape Cod. Benny, about to graduate from Harvard Business School, felt American companies treated him better than their Asian counterparts. They offered to fly him down for job interviews, give him full pay for summer internships and higher starting salaries. "Why should I lose money by going back?" he asked. We sat in his living room as he went through the list of companies who were offering big money for his services. "I wanted to go back home to work for a government-linked company this summer," he said. "With all this talk of regionalisation, I thought it might be worthwhile. You know what happened? They offered me the job, but then they said they could not pay me more than $200 a month. It's just an attachment, they said. American companies are willing to pay you a full salary. They know they are still paying you less than a consultant. And they are willing to spend and think long term."

Working and living in America has both personal and professional rewards. It offers cheap cars and houses, more leisure and quality time for spouse and family, the seasons and recreation, as well as career opportunities on par, if not ahead, of what Asia presently promises. In many fields – the financial community, science, technology and research, the arts, media and design – America still has strength and specialisation. The list is familiar but those who knock America may need a gentle reminder of them; despite problems like crime and violence, there is an American way of life, a cultural context, that still attracts.

Those who come will find ways to live with or apart from these concerns, whether in Chinatowns and ethnic neighbourhoods or in upper-class enclaves. Singaporeans especially, well-qualified and English-speaking like our friends Karen and Linus, will have recourse to private schools for their children and homes in safer suburbs. There remains the possibility of prejudice, however. According to one survey, more than 60 per cent of Americans thought there were already too many Asians. California, with the highest Asian population at more than three million, proposed strict new measures against illegal immigrants, aimed primarily at Hispanics, but of concern to Asians too. Asian professionals have reported a "glass ceiling" that prevents their advancement, especially in medicine and engineering. Despite the Statue of Liberty's invitation to the tired and hungry, newcomers cannot expect everything to be rosy upon arrival. Yet, despite it all, Asians still come westward.

There is an annual State Department lottery that randomly gives out Green Cards, conferring the right to stay in the USA. This is as popular as billion-dollar sweepstakes; thousands apply for the few cards that are available. Many even pay agencies who claim (falsely) to be able to help them. There are illegal immigrants hidden in the belly of container ships, risking trans-Pacific journeys, even with China's booming growth. There are Singaporeans who go, despite the nation's rapid growth and promise of personal safety. There are new immigrants who, once established, are quick to sponsor their relatives to join them. There are many like Ken who do not think of returning to Asia despite its resurgence and America's present frailties.

I met a third Asian who spoke about America beyond the economic rewards or the leisure of a five-day week. Hiroshi was a 21-year-old Japanese. He was born in Tokyo and came to America only at 18, for college. His spoken English was still a little rough after three years; he hardly knew a word before he thought of coming and even then struggled vainly with language tapes. But he fitted in with little problem. His hair was cut ultra-short at the back with a longer, wildly-gelled fringe on the top. He wore Doc Martens and torn jeans. His lean body was muscular from working out at the gym. He had become an expert roller-blader and, on weekends, served as a volunteer patrolman on the roller-blading path along the riverside. He stood tall on his roller-blades, cool in cut-off T-shirt and sunglasses.

"I love it here," he said, his accent equal parts Japanese staccato and American drawl. "I met a guy last weekend. He was in his late 40s. A senior manager in a bank. And you know what? He was learning to roller-blade. Can you imagine, a guy like that. You would never see that in Japan. I can't imagine my father trying to learn anything new like that. He wouldn't have the time. More than that, he wouldn't do it. It just wouldn't be accept-able."

The Japan Hiroshi described had a strict and narrow route: the right school and then the right university, all leading to a big company and steady progress up the escalator of success and salary. On that path, there was no riverside path for leisure, no place for senior executives to learn roller-blading. "Back home, there's no room for mistakes. You don't dare do anything different, in case you make a mistake. Here in America, you're free to do what you like. If you fail, you can always try again."

The place where Hiroshi and others roller-bladed was idyllic at sunset. The water ran by. There was the soft lawn for picnicking. Behind the people, the city of Boston was apparent but not intrusive. However, it is not just such scenes and sunny, good weather – like that day we had cycled with Ken – that have brought Asians and so many others to America. Even on bad and rainy days, in social and economic hard times, America and the American way of life, both reality and promise, still have their attractions.

❖

It was after a late summer day that I talked to Ken and Danna about the idea of race in America. There were just the four of us in their back yard. Ken wore faded jeans and a pullover against the slight chill of the evening. He grilled hamburgers on the BBQ. We sat at a picnic table, laid out with all the sauces and condiments. Danna told us how she used to work summers in a fast-food joint. The future doctor served as cheap labour, behind the counter in a paper hat and bib. The mustard, she learnt, was always spread against the meat patty. The mayo went between the lettuce and the bun. The first was to bring out the flavour of the meat; the second to moisten the bread. We tried it Danna's way and the home-made burgers were more delicious than anything you could get in a fast-food joint. The activities we liked – biking, camping, eating – had brought us to know each other well in the time we had been in the country. I had told Danna my stories about encountering Asian-Americans, African-Americans, Native Americans and other minorities. In writing my newspaper columns about America, Danna was the person I spoke with the most. She was American, after all, born and bred: White and born in a small town on the West Coast. And we had become friends. But the answer to my query about race came reluctantly at first.

"You mean like do we get noticed because we're a mixed couple?" Danna asked, tentatively.

"Yeah," Ken said as he put the burger into the fresh, sesame-topped bun and dressed it with lettuce, a slice of tomato and sauces. "Tell him about your grandfather."

"Oh, Ken."

"Tell him, tell him."

"Well, you tell him."

"The guy refuses to accept the fact that we're married."

"Well, he knows we're married. It just took him a long time to talk to you."

"He still doesn't talk to me."

"He does."

"But he makes it clear he doesn't like the fact that I'm Chinese. That's pretty clear."

"It's not that you're Chinese. It's just that you're not, you know, White."

"He was in the Klu Klux Klan, you know. Her grandfather was in it. You think the little town she grew up in was quiet and peaceful?"

"No, c'mon Ken. It was a quiet town. It's not that we lynched anybody. But you know, the nearest Black family was in the next county. The closest we got to a Chinese family was in the next town, where there was a take-away. Once a week or so, we would eat Chinese. My sister and I would order burgers or fried chicken. We just weren't used to people of any other race."

"Can you believe it? Chicken or burgers. That's what they ordered from a Chinese restaurant."

"But you know the strangest part, Ken?"

"Yeah, yeah. Tell them about that. That is so weird. Tell them, hon'."

"Well, I'm part Native American. Not much but my mother told me. I don't know what tribe or anything because we never talked about it. Never admitted it to anyone we knew in that town we grew up in."

"Part red Indian. And her grandfather was a member of the Klu Klux Klan."

"And now my husband's Chinese."

In the back yard of their home, with hot grilled burgers in front of them, Ken and Danna began debating their favourite question about which combination was more common in America: a White man with an Asian woman, or the reverse. He smiled abruptly before he bit into the delicious grilled burger. She held hers up into front of her face, waiting until she had stopped laughing.

country life

outside
the mainstream

LEAVING HARVARD It is impractical to wear a suit, black robes and a flat black hat in hot, late May. Especially when you have to spend a long time outdoors, crowded in by many others similarly dressed. But that is the tradition of commencement at Harvard when thousands of students from the college and from graduate schools of business, law, medicine and education get their degrees in the historic Harvard Yard. Grand occasion demands the ridiculous.

Commencement morning began with a champagne breakfast in a huge white tent set out on the lawns. Jin Hua and I wandered around, holding a plate of fruit that we shared. She wore a cheongsam, the most formal dress she brought to America and something that always elicited compliments. She drank a cup of tea. I was decked out in the full commencement regalia, champagne fortifying the silliness of the get-up. Everyone from my class was there. And, as on each occasion I saw them gathered, I was struck by their diversity of nationality and race. From Mexico and Latin America, from Canada, Australia and England, from Eastern and Western Europe, from Ghana, South Africa, Kenya and other countries in Africa, from Japan, Korea and China, from Indonesia, Thailand, Malaysia, the Philippines, Singapore and other parts of Asia: the law school had gathered these 100 or so foreign students in this one place. I knew many but not all of my classmates. I knew some but not many of the Americans who were in the three-year programme.

I had learnt my way around the large campus with its green lawns and old red brick buildings. I had gone beyond the law school to explore cavernous Widener Library and meet up with teachers and students in politics, the Kennedy School for Government and the department of anthropology. I had grown used to the place and the people. But I had never felt fully at home, never really a Harvard man.

After a year of study, coming to know the country and my American classmates, after commencement, I and all of my class would head back to where we had come from. On commencement morning, we assembled as one body for the last time and headed to Harvard Yard for the ceremony.

In the weeks approaching commencement, many had asked me if my family would be coming. Some were friends while others had hardly said a word to me the whole year. The question was not a matter of concern. It was that each graduate gets only three tickets for the commencement and extras are in short supply. Those with bigger families must then hope to find those who are on their own or, like me, accompanied only by one person. They can then beg for the extra tickets. There was a poster warning students that extra tickets could not be sold. Favours and meals, however, were sometimes traded. Offers deluged me until I pledged mine to a friend from Brazil. Then the interest in me and my family arrangements dwindled. That was very much Harvard as I knew it. Not a warm community, but a collection of bright people who believed they were on the way up, with all the networking, perks and deal-making that came with it. The neo-classical buildings and ivy league demeanour only disguised the grasping.

The Yard is a grassy space between the huge neo-classical Widener library and a church with an elegant spire, and flanked on the sides by other, smaller buildings. It is open except for a few tall trees, easily large enough for a football game. On most days, it is quiet and pleasant to stroll through on the way to the library with its broad steps, like approaching a Roman temple. At commencement, the Yard spilled over with people. Those graduating – almost 6,000 – perched on rows of chairs in the black robes, squeezed tight together. Those watching sat high above, on benches placed on the library steps. Jin Hua was up there, so far away that I could not see her. I was lost to her too, in the sea of black robes in the Yard. I sat between my classmate from China, Xiao Bing, and another from Canada, Kerry. Jin Hua was with Xiao Bing's wife, Yuen Ping, and Kerry's sister. I had come to know Xiao Bing and Kerry better than most other people at Harvard. Like me, they were interested in international events and law and had come back to school in their 30s; they also had a sense of humour and enjoyed good food. Shared interests helped us bridge something of the cultural and other gaps. My position between them also seemed fitting at a symbolic level: in many ways, through the year, I felt very much in between Xiao Bing from mainland China and Kerry from the English-speaking West.

Around us, groups shouted out their cheers. Those from the college, mostly undergrads, were in the centre of things and made the most noise. The business school was also raucous, notorious for celebrating the graduation by throwing dollar notes into the air. The law school, slightly off to the left, was quieter. Until the ceremony began, Xiao Bing, Kerry and others around me contented ourselves with conversation and taking snapshots of the moment. At about 10 am, the sheriff of Middlesex County called us to order. With a prayer led by the university chaplain, Harvard's 343rd commencement began. A church anthem and Latin salutary followed. I, from Singapore, was impressed by the antiquity and arcane rituals. A classmate later revealed a different perspective. His university in Germany dated from the 16th century and, he snorted, the speaker's Latin was all wrong.

Two representatives of the graduating class spoke. The first exhorted the graduates to be something, to do something good for America. The second spoke about the next goal in business, in society, in this country; he imagined a world in which one can be in New York and do business with California. Their exhortations were echoed by the commencement speaker, Vice-President Al Gore, that afternoon. Gore, from the Harvard class of 1969, spoke about where the country had gone since those heady days. He called on the graduating class to believe in hope over despair, drive over resignation, and faith over cynicism. The sentiments were universal, but the context and the emphasis were particularly American.

Returning to the grounds of the law school, I joined my classmates to wait our turn to receive our degrees from the dean. A representative from the class gave another speech, also about America. I stood among the 100 or so gathered from countries all over the world. When the speech was over, we paraded up the stage for the scroll. As each of us came onto the stage, it was mainly the other international students who applauded, not the Americans. Afterwards, we talked among ourselves about other things in our different countries, in the international community. Xiao Bing and Kerry congratulated me on receiving an award, the law school's Laylin Prize. Xiao Bing thought it was appropriate that it be for international law; the Americans won the prizes for the subjects that concerned their national laws. Those were their priorities, Kerry said, those were the laws that were going to land them the $200,000-a-year jobs in New York.

We laughed among ourselves. A few other friends joined us: Juan from Mexico and his wife Gloria, Luiz from Brazil, Ephraim from Nigeria, Melli from Indonesia, Stella and Paul from Australia, Jonas from Belgium. Some of us would head back home right after commencement. Others were staying on for a few months to work in a law firm, to study for the New York bar. A few planned longer-term, to stay on for another degree or a full-time job. Harvard was their entry into America. A more elite institution than the Chinatowns and ethnic ghettos where other foreigners made their transition, but the university served much the same function. It was here that we learned the craft and language. It was here that we earned our provisional acceptance into society. A bright young student from elsewhere would find it hard to find a job in America. The same person, a year later and with a Master's from this university, found it easier. Some, in fact, got the Manhattan jobs that Americans also wanted. For many of those who were headed home too, the degree meant something special: greater job opportunities, better contacts and belonging to a reputable alma mater. Despite its shortcomings, few universities in America and the world could match Harvard for that all-important quality: brand-name recognition.

I did not go back immediately after graduation. Nor did I go into the American mainstream to cash in on my degree at Wall Street. Jin Hua had still to finish another semester for her Master's at Boston University. I would stay on as a visiting fellow in a small institution nearby that focused on ethnic issues around the world. I would also assist two professors with research projects. Then, in the fall, we would leave Cambridge at the end of our house lease. We would look for a quiet place nearby, where Jin could complete the writing of her thesis and I would begin writing a new book of stories.

We were leaving the mainstream: I sensed it even on that commencement day. The class would disperse. Harvard would not be the same place. For me, the series of talks and seminars would stop. The classrooms and libraries would be empty. Faces that had become familiar would be absent in the corridors.

But whether we stayed or went, we were always in a minority at the university. Even if, in class, when gathered together with so many other non-Americans, we did not feel it, the commencement exercise had shown that. Beneath the cosmopolitan surface of the university and Cambridge, in the speeches with all their references to the country, in seeing the 6,000 graduates in one place for the first time, its American nature and the predominantly White atmosphere had become clear. With our robes and scrolls, we were acceptable for a while. But we were still aliens, guests in someone's home. All of us, and all the wider world we represented, were just an island in America's vast continent. It was time for us all to leave Harvard. For Jin and I, we would head for new and different parts of America.

THE GREAT OUTDOORS On a coast in Maine a trail leads through woods to a rocky promontory. "No radios or loud parties," warned Mike, who ran Ocean Woods. "This is a wilderness area." He gave us a map and took our $4 for the camping site. We nodded and began our hike. The deep ocean waves crashed against the rocks. As the water retreated, the stones on the shore rattled. Above us, the sea birds swirled and cried. The sea wind breathed through the pine and birch trees. We would be content with these sounds, an isolated camp-site for our two-person tent and a simple open fire. No radios or loud parties: that was the point of coming here, into what Americans call the "Great Outdoors".

The escape from Harvard and the city was easy enough. That is part of the appeal of America: tired of urban life, you can always jump into your car and get away from it all. The trick is knowing where to go. From our home in Cambridge, a four-lane highway took us straight north. We exited for a small town near the coast, taking the narrow but well-paved road to Acadia National Park. The park is perhaps the prime wilderness escape on the rugged Northeast coast. Made from gifts of land from rich families, it comprises different sections of three separate headlands on adjacent peninsulas, not one enormous spread of land like most other national parks. Acadia is also one of the most popular parks. Between that relatively small size and the large crowds, the main section at Bar Harbour can be distinctly crowded in summer. Around the fourth of July, hiking is more like taking a stroll through a city park rather than the wilderness – the sights are enjoyable enough but you are never quite alone. But where we were headed, the most northern section of the park on the Schoodic peninsula, things were quieter, even in the thrall of summer.

Where to camp is just as important. Some campgrounds are little more than glorified carparks. They offer spots for the tent and car, separated from the next site by only a few yards and some trees. Only a minority, like Ocean Woods, allow more space and unobstructed views; a bigger and better slice of the Great Outdoors. The trade-off is the lack of conveniences. Wilderness sites, unlike others, do not offer nearby showers and toilets, swimming pools or electrical outlets. There is choice and luxury in all things in this country, even its wilderness. We opted for the no-frills wilderness.

The trek into the camp was quite long. By the time we had finished carrying up our things and set up the tent, we felt hot. We walked down a steep but short path down to the pebble beach. We waded out into the clear water, too cold for swimming but refreshing against the heat of summer. After settling in, we set off to bike a 15-mile trail along the coast. We enjoyed a lunch from the simple provisions we had carried with us. I gathered fallen wood for a fire, for cooking and to provide light in the evening. On this stretch of rocky coast, we felt as if we were the only people in the world. Who needs electrical outlets? Who wants loud music and partying?

Later, when we walked to the showers in another section of the campground, we met those who did. Campers arrived with four-wheel-drive jeeps and RVs, recreational vehicles, enormous things equipped like town apartments on wheels, with built-in kitchens, showers, beds and other amenities. A thick cable from each RV plugged into an outlet behind a bush, providing electricity to run everything. The bare-bodied campers lounged in deck chairs, radios, allowed in this area, booming. Father adjusted the portable TV while two sons whined about the poor reception. Beer was flowing.

Campers nodded and greeted us as we passed from one site to the next. There was a relaxed party atmosphere on this side of the camp.

"Great view, ain't it," one bellowed good-heartedly, gesturing at the ocean.

"Isn't this the life?" the next exclaimed, smiling broadly.

"Where are you from?" a small woman in a big sun hat asked. "Would you like a drink?"

We smiled, but shook our heads and walked on. As I waited for Jin Hua to finish her shower, sitting outside on a bench, conversation was inevitable. "I'm waiting for my wife too," Dave started, establishing a common point. "Women always take longer. Even when they're camping, they gotta make sure their hair looks right. Isn't that the funniest thing?" He laughed heartily. He was a big man in his late 30s or early 40s, with reddish skin that seemed sunburnt.

"Is this your first time here? We come every year. Been coming since the place started. Mike's great. You met Mike, right, the owner? We love camping, the whole family, and this is our favourite place. It's not too crowded, you know. And you can't beat the views." In the five minutes before Jin Hua came out, we introduced ourselves, told each other what we did. I learnt the names of Dave's wife and kids. I knew they lived in a suburb, in a house with a big lawn. Dave often BBQ'd in the back yard. Sherry, his wife, tended to the flowers. The son, Scott, mowed the lawn for a small fee. Dave was born on a farm in Connecticut, now overgrown by suburbs and malls. His wife hailed from New Hampshire.

He worked for an insurance company in New Haven. Desk-bound but, he repeated several times, he still loved the outdoors and getting away from it all.

We had gotten to know each other. Then Jin Hua came out from the shower and we parted. We each genuinely wished the other a good weekend, although we would never meet again beyond that place or time. It felt strange to me. As I walked away, I could hear Dave begin a conversation with someone else, also waiting outside the showers.

Americans are a friendly but transient people. Greetings are exchanged. Drinks offered. Conversations struck up. The camp was a community on wheels. Our common interests in camping, in the wilderness around us, in waiting for a spouse outside the shower, bound us together for a while. Then, as easy as the first hello and exchange of life stories, we separated. America is a continent, not just a country. Its borders, moreover, have been unfolding, stretching. As the historian Frederick Turner pointed out, the American frontier only closed in the late 19th century, with the settling of California. Before that, for centuries, there was a continuing expansion westwards.

This size and delayed recognition of borders and limits affect the American psyche. One of the effects is the immediacy of American friendliness. Another is the idea that you can escape from it all. You can exchange one city for another. You can exchange countryside for city, city for suburbs, suburbs for the Great Outdoors. If you don't like one place, or if there is too much crime or pollution, you can always go somewhere else. The idea of space and resources being finite, limited, is virtually non-existent. This can be seen in their attitudes to nature.

Americans often bring up the outdoor life. They fondly remember summer camps or a family farm, and regularly go camping, whether in an RV or tent. Like Dave and his family, they relish leaving the city to get away from it all. Even in the suburbs, they lovingly weed and tend their green lawns, bringing flowers into colourful bloom. At a broader level, they can often talk about oil spills and wax lyrical about disappearing rainforests and endangered whales. Such sentiments are usually meant sincerely. Many American individuals and organisations try to solve environmental problems across the world. But there are many shades of green in America.

While some call for the protection of tropical rainforests and endangered species, others in the Pacific Northwest are felling old-growth trees, and ranchers are calling for the native wolf to be exterminated because it threatens their livestock. The pleasant lawns of suburbia are bought at a high cost. Motorised lawnmowers spew 11 times more smog than typical cars and account for five per cent of air pollution; American homes spend some $7 billion a year on planting, maintenance and pesticides of their lawns; and some regions, especially in the dry Southwest, use 30–60 per cent of their water supply just to keep the lawns green. The four-wheel-drive jeeps in which Americans come to this camp, to the wilderness, guzzle gasoline. The American lifestyle and attitude to the environment are often ambivalent and contradictory.

Most Americans, it seems, neither want to destroy the environment nor to leave it in a natural state. Their inclination is to enjoy nature, but first they want to make it safe and convenient. Typically, such campers don't really get away from it all; they bring much of it with them. This habit may be ingrained. Historians tell us that the earliest Pilgrim settlers were unsettled by the forest lands they found so much darker and wilder than the tidier landscapes of Europe. Decades of settling, clearing and mining followed: some nine-tenths of American forests fell. Lumberjacks, like Paul Bunyan, became folk heroes. Even when conservation started in this country, a motivation of President Teddy Roosevelt was to ensure there would still be some wildlife to shoot – and he didn't mean with a camera.

Despite growing environmental awareness, there remains the idea in the American consciousness that nature is there for their use. From these roots, a movement known as Wise Use has grown in recent years to oppose higher environmental standards and support continuing government subsidies for logging, farming, mining and any number of industries that live off America's still bountiful natural resources.

Although backed by big industry, Wise Use has associated itself with images of the little guy – the family farmer or rancher, loggers in jackboots – whose livelihood needs protection from environmentalists who are portrayed as over-educated, urban-based, yuppie eco-lovers. This message struck a chord with many. When, for example, environmentalists tried to stop logging to save the habitat of the spotted owl on the Pacific

Northwest coast, public opinion turned against them. People put aside their concern for wildlife because of the potential loss of jobs. The change of attitude shows the practicality that is an integral part of the American character. Another recurring idea is that nature is there for a purpose, for use.

Back at our camp site, Mike, the camp manager, came by on his rounds. We invited him to sit down for a cold drink. He told us about the area, the types of trees. He also told us about the work of running the camp and making a living. He spoke slowly, not talking much about himself. But he said that the camp was part of a larger project, started by a friend of his, with part of the profits put to good use in small-scale projects for villages in Central America and the Pacific, to help the poor and protect the environment.

"That is one of the best things, to know that what I'm doing helps somewhere else too. And this is the best part of Ocean Woods, right here." His voice was quiet against the sound of the sea and the wind in the trees. But if he felt that way, I asked, why does the campground also cater to RVs? He grinned, shrugged and gave a sign known all over America and the world, one that environmentalists and nature-lovers must also contend with: his thumb and forefinger rubbing against each other. Money – there are different shades of green. "Besides," he continued, "there are plenty with families who couldn't enjoy it otherwise. It's still better to have some woods than none at all. They aren't disturbing you, are they?"

I listened. But there were no engines or radios or raucous laughter; nothing beyond the sounds of nature.

No, I shook my head, nothing disturbed me. After Mike left, we cooked lobsters. We had bought them from a shack on a tiny pier between the camp and the nearest town from an old couple who even lent us a pot to boil them in. They were beautiful hard-shell lobsters and, boiled on an open fire, in ocean water, brought a luxury to our time in the woods. We talked about the old couple in the lobster shack.

He was a small, balding man, red from working in the sun. She wore curlers in her hair and, weighing over 200 pounds, could hardly get out the door of their small house. They both spoke in such thick Maine accents that we hardly understood a word, but their kindness was clear. We would return their lobster pot the next morning and they had promised to show us a route to explore the coast. This was why we had come to this quieter part of Maine: for the beauty of its rocky shoreline and to encounter its people.

We watched the sun go down on the sea's wide, clear horizon. The stars started to show. A cool wind blew. After dinner, I walked down to the sea to use the rough sand to clean off most of the black soot that the open fire had deposited on the pot. Later, washing up for an early night's sleep, we headed up to the showers again. When we passed an RV on the way back, someone looked up briefly.

"Lovely out here, isn't it?" he said above the loud music. Jin Hua and I just nodded.

OLD HIPPIES NEVER DIE The week after we returned from camping in Maine, Mei Ping called. She was a writer, born in Malaysia but now settled in America. We had met when she and her husband, Peter, were in Singapore, teaching at the university before returning to work in a college near Philadelphia. We kept in touch by phone and the occasional postcard, but had yet to meet up. This was our chance. They went to stay on their farm, a place named Pingsbrooke, for the summer. It was some three hours' drive north of us, in Vermont.

"Come up for a few days," Mei suggested. We agreed with little hesitation. Peter came on the phone to give directions in his gravelly, country-blues voice.

"From Boston, head for the northeast and Saint Johnsbury. But don't go into town. Get on Route 93, right to the end. Get onto Route 91, head north for two-tenths of a mile. Get off at Exit 20, yes, Exit 20. Take Route 5 south, two miles to Passumpsic. There's nothing much in town. There's a sharp turn to the left, across from a church with a steeple. There's a Mobil station at the village store. Oh, but that's closed now. Then, about 200 yards on the left, next to the red barn, there's a sign that says 'Hidden Drive'. The road goes uphill, becomes dirt, flattens out, and then goes past farmland. There's a right-hand fork – don't take it. Bear left. Go about a mile. The road descends rapidly. There's a barn that says '1896', a pond. The road goes down steep. There's a four-corners (that's what they call a cross junction in these parts). Bear right. At the bottom, go across the brook. Go up the high hill, dip down again, then on the left, there's a puddle-like pond and a mail-box for the farm. The drive leading in is on the right. Go up, oh, about one-third of a mile and you're there."

He laughed when he finished. Peter had told so many friends over the years that the directions had become a recitation, almost a song. He should submit it to the *New Yorker*, some of his friends had suggested; it typified the kind of instructions that take you off the road, to a summer house in the countryside. Unused to such typical American things, I wondered if we would find our way to Pingsbrooke. Don't worry, Peter – having been in Singapore – assured us, it's easier than finding your way through HDB new towns.

A few days later, we headed out in our little Honda. We had packed our camping things and loaded our bicycles on a rear rack. We had also prepared ourselves mentally. Vermont has a very different mind-set from most states in the USA, let alone urban Singapore. It is one of the least populated states and one of the greenest. Stretches of forest still earn its original name in French, Vert Mont, or "green mountain". It is also a known retreat for old hippies and others tired of city life.

It was in Vermont that two old hippies took a $5 correspondence course and started selling ice-cream from an abandoned gas station. They now have annual sales of $140 million and employ 600 people. Ben Cohen and Jerry Warfield's gourmet ice-cream is publicly listed and a household name across America: Ben & Jerry's. Theirs is an American success story, an example for Horatio Alger and others who affirm that this is the land of opportunity and repeat the refrain "only in America". But with a twist.

Ben & Jerry's corporate HQ sits not in New York or a big city but in the otherwise quiet town of Waterbury, just off the winding, one-lane Route 100 in northern Vermont. We stopped there, some way from

Pingsbrooke. It was not a grand or imposing tower; more like a children's fun fair. Colourful tents sold T-shirts, mugs, plastic models of the typical black and white cows, and of course ice-cream. An area with picnic tables was labelled "Loafing area (Employees Only)". Inside, corporate dress was not shirt-and-tie but seemed to be tie-dye T-shirts. In the gift shop, posters encouraged you to recycle and save the planet. Employees moved around, busy but smiling, almost all young.

The company competes with Häagen-Dazs to be America's top luxury ice-cream brand. It is a market that is worth many millions but Ben & Jerry's wears its hippie roots and social causes as a badge of difference. Hence, the flavour "Cherry Garcia" takes its name from the leader of legendary 1960s hippie band, Grateful Dead, Jerry Garcia. And "Rainforest Crunch" is ice-cream with brazil nuts from tropical jungles to encourage the sustainable harvest of such products, instead of logging. The company donates 7.5 per cent of earnings to world peace, poor children and other causes. In business too, it supports and buys products from local cooperatives of smaller, family-owned farms and bakeries that employ the homeless and recovering alcoholics. Bottom line at the top: Ben, founder and CEO, is paid not more than seven times than the lowest-paid employee; other American corporate heads get million-dollar salaries and private jets.

For such reasons, some small conservative factions in America boycott Ben & Jerry's as "communist ice-cream". While it is clearly a capitalist undertaking, the company does exemplify socially-conscious hippies who

came to Vermont in the 1970s. Many have also found
success, albeit on a smaller scale, in farming, arts and
crafts, gourmet cheese-making and other undertakings.
They have slowly won their place among the older
established and more conservative Vermont folks. Yet
many ex-hippies maintain their principles by, for example, making their farms organic or refusing to log their
land.

They have helped many fields and pasture lands in
Vermont grow back to woods and give the state more
greenery and greater environmental protection than
most places in America. But just as hippies can become
millionaires and farms turn back into forest, future
change is also possible – and not always for the better.

When we were in Vermont, profits and share prices
were down at Ben & Jerry's for the first time. They were
looking for a new CEO, according to the newspapers.
Ben, as founder, would retain his shares and continue as
chairman to keep the original spirit of the place. But for
the business itself, competition for market share and
expansion abroad required business school savvy. The
change was one of principle too: the new CEO would
receive a top-draw salary, unrestricted by the old limit
of seven times the lowest pay. If other things changed,
like its quirky corporate culture and social programme,
Ben & Jerry's might become just another big corporation. That was what some commentators worried
about. The happy era of mixing of hippie values and
commerce was under attack, for them and others of
their generation. Signs were visible in the green Vermont hills.

Walking in the dense, cool woods, we were startled. Not by the deer, raccoons or bears which lived here but by an area where they could not live. There, over some 50 acres, all the trees had been clear-cut. The reddish soil, ripped up by tractors, was littered with stumps, up-ended roots and the toppled remains of less valuable trees. When the rain came, the soil would wash away and silt up a nearby stream. "They clear-cut part of their land," Peter explained the action of a neighbour. "The loggers made them an offer that was too good to turn down." To some, unemployment rates higher than in city areas combined with rising timber prices to make logging more attractive than before.

The situation repeated itself across Vermont and, indeed, many other states. Loggers and pro-business factions argued for jobs and profits; others spoke up for aesthetics, loss of animal habitat and water supply. On a nearby mountain, some 1,500 acres were clear-cut, despite protests. Tourism and summer home projects also called for the land to be cleared. The right balance between these different needs was still unresolved. I nodded when Peter talked about the lack of jobs in the area, understanding pragmatism in hard times. But part of me was still struck, almost viscerally, by the contrast of the clear-cut land to the surrounding woods. Thankfully, there were many other areas that were still green, inviolate.

Peter and Mei walked us across their land. Their daughter Marian and Cloud, their dog, rushed on ahead. When they were uncertain of the way, they would wait for Peter, tall and wearing a red bandanna across his forehead. We followed more slowly with Mei, carrying our things for a swim in the stream and, afterwards, a picnic on the banks. The path led steeply downhill through the woods and then opened out onto a field of shoulder-high grass. The edge of each blade of grass was sharp and the path less certain. We just needed to push through to the stream.

It was clear and shallow. There were some rocks and branches of trees that had fallen over trailed in the water. But, in one part, the water was deep and cold on that hot summer day. We swam there. Then we sat on the picnic mat, surrounded by the tall grass, until the sun had dried us. We ate a little of the bread, cold cuts and sandwiches that had been carried in a big woven basket. There was a bottle of wine that we drank from and then placed in the stream to keep cool.

After that, Peter produced a small can of worms and two rods. We went off to another section of the stream to fish. He had spent a year among Native Americans as part of his studies in anthropology, learning how to fish in the process. He told us to move quietly as we got near the water, or otherwise the fish would sense us and move on. I tried but the grass rustled around me. Peter himself moved quietly for such a big man. On the bank, he spotted two fish under a half-submerged log. The current in the brook was fast and they had found this spot outside the mainstream, beyond the swirl of things, in the shade. They were small but full-grown brook trout, Peter explained, and very tasty. He cast the line and handed the rod over to Jin. Then he did another for me. He whispered instructions for us to wait until we sensed the fish bite and then yank the line tight. I tried but got none and tangled the line. Peter took over and caught two. Jin Hua surprised everyone by landing four, flapping bright silver in the sun. With that catch, we walked on, took another dip and then headed up to the house.

Six fish was enough for dinner and that was what we had that evening in Pingsbrooke. The brook trout were pan-fried, with salt and some lemon. Vegetables came from the small, organic garden Mei and Peter had grown, including zucchini flowers which Mei fried in batter. I prepared the salad and pasta that rounded up the meal, filling in the spots of hunger that the delicious but small fish missed. Except for the pasta, everything had come from the farm itself.

It was dark by the time dinner was over. We sat on the wooden porch in front of the house, outdoors, under the stars. We talked about $135 tickets for Woodstock II and the revival of 1960s fashion among today's youth that some saw as commercial rip-offs and pale imitations. Mei and Peter were of that original generation, students in the late 1960s and 1970s, against the war. They had seen the changes in America and spoke of old times wistfully. We also talked about Ben & Jerry's and the clear-cut logging we had seen earlier. They also knew of these things, and more changes that were coming. Then my friends told me that loggers had come to survey their land too.

Peter rubbed his bearded chin and assured us that they had refused clear-cutting, although the money was tempting. What they would, however, consider was selective logging. Some of the trees would be cut in an area, with enough left to retain the greenery and protect against soil erosion. The woods were thick enough for that, if done carefully. The land at Pingsbrooke large enough so no one would notice. Such a compromise would allow logging and bring in income. While some damage would result, much of the land and greenery would remain, leaving animals a place to live. Having walked the land and swum in the stream, I was relieved.

In the 1960s, hippies may have criticised any compromise as "selling out". That, and trusting anyone older than 30, were the great evils of their generation. But now they have grown older, some are landowners and job-holders, like Peter and Mei. Others like Ben Cohen and Jerry Warfield are stockholders and entrepreneurs. They have sought a balance.

In Vermont, they live next to country people. In this, there is some accommodation. Between those who traditionally hunt and the newcomers like Mei for whom it is an abhorrent blood sport. Between those who farm the land with pesticides and chemical fertilisers and ex-hippies who favour organic farms. Between those who log trees and some, like Peter and Mei's neighbours, who run a bookstore that stocks Marquez, Achebe and many of the better American writers. It is not confrontation and noisy rebellion that those who moved into Vermont sought. Those things were left behind when they left the city. Most have, instead, sought a way of holding on to their principles and still getting by, getting on with their lives, in peace.

For corporations and capitalists of what they used to call "the establishment", the answer has always been obvious, uncompromising: maximise logging, building and profits. To do anything less might, for some, seem insufficiently American. Perhaps the remarkable thing about Ben and Jerry and some of that hippie generation who have made it, is not that they have "grown up" with success, but that they still question those seemingly clear-cut answers.

On the porch at Pingsbrooke, we talked on. About America and about Asia. About a thousand small and big things from the neighbouring farms to the requisites of art: sometimes questioning, at other times laughing. Then it was almost ten, late by the standards of rural America, and we went to bed. The next morning, after a country breakfast of pancakes and bacon, all topped with the smoky, made-in-Vermont maple syrup, we began the drive home.

It was only a three-hour drive. Just three days had passed. But at Pingsbrooke, time moved differently and perceptions changed, like a spot outside the swirl of the brook that bordered the land. When we returned to our house at 32 Winslow Street in Cambridge, our back yard – previously a refuge enjoyed in all seasons – seemed suddenly small. All around us, everything was noisy and bustling.

a nation of
small towns

RETURNING TO VERMONT At the end of summer, our lease on 32 Winslow Street ran out. Jin Hua had still to write her thesis to finish her Master's program. We knew it would not be easy to find accommodation for a few short months. There was, moreover, no need to stay in the city; with sufficient research and occasional trips to her supervisor and the library, she could write her thesis somewhere else. We planned to rent a holiday bungalow for a few months, off-season on Cape Cod. The quiet and space by the sea would be conducive to work.

Our neighbour, Hilary Hopkins, had recommended a small group of chalets that they went to each summer, just yards from a quiet beach that faced out to the ocean. She had called the owner to let him know about us. It was a place for regulars and recommended friends; the old couple that ran the place didn't let out the small tidy bungalows to just anyone. We were to go out for a weekend visit. If we liked it and they liked us, we would agree on terms for the quiet fall months. But then Mei called.

They were leaving Vermont to return south to Philadelphia, where both she and Peter taught in colleges. Pingsbrooke would be empty for a few months until they decided what to do with it. It was fully furnished, down to pots and pans. There were food basics that we could help ourselves to as well as cacti and succulents that needed watering. The leaves would be turning colour on the land. They might come up for a few days to visit, otherwise, the house could be all ours until December. We had looked forward to the beach bungalow, imagining long walks on the sand and the sound of the waves and the salt-smell. But the three summer days we had spent at Pingsbrooke had only whetted our appetite for more. There was little question what our preference was. More or less immediately, we said, "Yes, thank you, Mei."

But leaving was not easy. After a year, we had accumulated a household. Some things we decided to ship home, including the first thing we had bought, our travelling trunk. Most of everything else was put on sale. With Jin Hua's experience of past garage sales, we emulated that American tradition. Hand-written signs were posted along the road, on notice boards at the supermarkets and in the universities. Prices were tagged on each item, big like the bed or small like a set of wine glasses. With help from our friends, especially Jin Hua's Japanese classmate Mami and fellow Singaporean Madge, things got done. By the end of the weekend sale, the house was as empty as the day we found it. Our pockets were pleasantly fuller than usual with money. We had got back a fair proportion of what we had spent, after a year of use.

We said our farewells to our neighbours, exchanging addresses with the Hopkinses and with Barbara and Edna up the street. We argued with our landlord, the lawyer Richard Rudman, because he wanted the house professionally cleaned when we had left it a far better state than when we had moved in. Perhaps the warmth we shared with our neighbours broke the stereotype of the cool and inscrutable Asian. Certainly, the resilience and vehemence in our arguments with Rudman confounded the image of the passive Asian. Jin Hua's anger especially, shattered the idea of the silent Asian wife.

It was therefore with a mix of resentment and sentiment that we got into our car, ready to drive out of Winslow Street. The house was vacant, already becoming distant in our minds. Our small Honda was full of bags, books and groceries, especially Chinese food-stuff that we imagined we could not get in Vermont. It seemed a modern, Asian version of the wagons in which American families had made the journey across the continent. We looked forward to a new place. And, like true aliens, we left nothing behind to mark our one year in that place. Although we were to come back to Cambridge in the months ahead, we never returned to the street on which we had once been neighbours and No. 32, the house that had been home.

AROUND THESE PARTS *Go right to the end of the highway, get off and head south on Route 5 until you reach Passumpsic. Just past where the gas station used to be, turn left. Then the dirt road begins. Travel on for three miles, up and down hills.*

Again, I drove off the broad, straight highways into a town that was just a small, insignificant blip on the vast map of America. According to that map, the dirt road I travelled did not even exist. The local map that showed the way, hand-drawn by Mei and Peter for our summer visit, was somewhere in the car boot. I proceeded from the memory of those short-long summer days. Tentative at first, uncertain if the left turn should be a right. Then, with a growing familiarity.

Pingsbrooke was set on some 150 acres of woods in hills above the town. The house was a modern but simple structure. There was no electricity unless the generator is running. The water came from a spring, capped to sustain pressure so it ran through the pipes. The house faced out, looking gently downhill to where our friends had planted the vegetable garden, next to the remaining foundation stones of a barn. Then steeper, down into a valley where the river we had swum and fished in ran. From the living room of Pingsbrooke, or the porch, you could look out across the valley to distant hill tops. No other home could be seen. None of the homes you saw on the way in, along the unpaved rural road. Nothing of the town below.

We spent the first day at Pingsbrooke in this solitude, taking in the space and quiet. Unpacking and getting used to things. On the second day, we went out for groceries and to see something of the surrounding area. Passumpsic, the place nearest Pingsbrooke, had just a few houses, small farms, two churches and a post-office. The gas station closed down for lack of business. A saw-mill struggled on. The town stretched out, along the winding, one-lane road for about a mile. Then, past a historical and unusual circular wooden barn, you would have left the town. There was nothing more. There was no grocery store. The nearest place for that was about ten miles away, in East Barnet – one of three villages that, with Passumpsic, made up the county of Barnet.

We stopped there, parking in one of the five car lots, across from the town-hall cum post office that is run by one clerk. The East Barnet general store sells everything from bread and fresh beef to shotgun ammo and the *New York Times*. We picked up some locally-made multi-grain bread and the local paper. The man in the general store greeted us, quiet but friendly. His accent was unusual, not something you heard on TV, the mainstream depictions of America. I found it hard at first to understand what he said. But there was no one else in the store and, as he packed our groceries slowly, went on talking. Eventually, I began to understand his twang. When we asked questions, he answered expansively.

We're new to the area, he knew. How long would we be staying? Three months, we replied: not so short that we were just another couple of the crowd of weekenders who came up from the city, but not so long that we were settlers, neighbours in a place that was 99 per cent White American. He seemed comfortable with that. He told us about the place he called "these here parts" and recounted the flood before the war. He told us about some places to hike in the hills. He let us know that the fall festivals were coming up, when each small town would hold an event in celebration. On that particular day, he told us we could watch a parade in another town nearby, Groton. The meaning of "nearby" to him was nearly 30 miles across another mountain in the Green Mountains range around which Barnet, Passumpsic and the Pingsbrooke house nestled.

The parade in Groton was mustered by the townfolk. Out of a population of 702, the volunteer fire service drove a 1950s firetruck, the boys marched as scouts, a family of five dressed up as clowns and a woman rode a horse in British-style riding outfit. All the while, the band from the district high school played "Rock around the Clock", one of two tunes in its repertoire. There were no fireworks and no large and glittering floats. But the crowd that lined the street was enthusiastic. They had come to cheer on a brother, an aunt, a cousin. One white-haired lady told me she knew "almost everyone" in the parade. It was a local celebration and a celebration of what and whom was local.

I was very far away from New York, LA and other large cities we usually picture when we think of America. The distance was more than geographic. Small-town USA is a state of mind. It is, according to many, where the American spirit is best found. This is the friendly, small-town spirit celebrated by dramatist Thornton Wilder in the 1938 play, *Our Town*. These are the face-to-face relations and the sense of community that led De Tocqueville, in his 19th-century classic *Democracy in*

America, to celebrate small towns as the best unit for democratic government.

In such a setting, we – in our out-of-state foreign-made car, with our alien, non-American passports and our Asian faces – were out of place. Yet, we were welcome. When one person asked "whereabouts" we were from, and we said Singapore, she asked which state that was in. When I explained that it was in Asia, her husband recalled something of the recent controversies between our countries. But it was curiosity and not ill-will that followed. We had to sign their visitors' book, another insisted. They liked to see from how far away some have come to their town. Once, they told us, someone came from London. If England was far away to them, I thought, Asia must have been unimaginable. They asked us what life was like there, in Asia. When that was done, we took our turn to ask about life in their area, "these parts".

We found that many were born in the town. Those who weren't, lived there or in other towns nearby for more than 20 years. Most had jobs in Saint Johnsbury, over the hills, the biggest town around. It was in Saint Johnsbury that people from all the surrounding small towns went to shop, to fill up their cars with gas and to work. That was a place we came to know fairly well, making two or three trips a week there for the super-market and newspaper. There was no place for Chinese supplies, but the supermarkets had good beef and local lamb, and reasonable seafood from nearby Maine. Sometimes we would catch a movie in the tiny cinema or pick up a video to watch.

There was a well-known school, the Academy, and the Green Mountain Mall which housed the big department store, JC Penny's. There were three supermarkets, three video stores and four gas stations. There was Northern Lights, the bookstore and café, two health food stores and a bagel shop. There was a museum and a weather station that gave meteorological forecasts, as the weather could be very changeable in the mountain region. Perhaps the highlight of the town was the Athenaeum, a public library of wood and brick that went back to the 19th century, and boasted a conservatory with antique furniture and a large mural by an early American painter.

Yet even there in Saint Johnsbury, people recognised and greeted each other in the street: a sign that it remained a small town, not a city. The big economic debate was not whether America should approve the new GATT round and open up to world trade, which happened that year. It was whether to allow the big chain store Wal-Mart to set up shop in Saint Johnsbury. Some said it would help their sluggish economy; others that this would ruin local businesses that could not offer the volume and low prices of the giant chain. The local newspapers were full of the debate, even if the *New York Times* brought them news on issues of the larger, metropolitan world beyond.

It was in Saint Johnsbury that the farmer's market was held, every Saturday from summer to fall. At the market, farmers displayed their produce for sale directly to their customers, promising slightly lower prices than the supermarkets and, moreover, offered fresh produce without chemicals. We were familiar with the institution, having been regulars at one in Cambridge. The one in Saint Johnsbury was in the car park, next to the school, across from a gas station. It was a small affair with ten-or-so stalls of produce, and some others selling knitwear and handicraft. We walked around, surveying what was on offer that was not planted in the garden at Pingsbrooke. By the third week, the stall holders smiled at us, knowing that we were not just weekenders, but there for a slightly longer term.

Among them, there was a single African-American farmer. He would not stand out in the cities but in this rural area, in the north, there were few of his race. His was the only stall which sold mustard greens, a pungent vegetable that is often used in southern cooking but is very seldom seen in Vermont. He told us how it could be used for cooking and we talked for a while. I began to tell him that we stayed around the area, but he told us that he has already heard something about it. I had told the bookstore owners and, after filling the car for the second week, the gas station owner. We had contacted Mei and Peter's friends in the area to say hello, and begun to shop at RJ's, their usual butchers at the corner. Notice of us moving into town, I realised, must have spread. Two Asians in a small red Honda stood out a little in these parts; as did a Black farmer with mustard greens.

"It doesn't take much to get noticed around here," the farmer said. "People are used to knowing just who everyone is. If you move in, they're going to want to know. Even if you're White like them. They'll say something like, 'So-and-so has moved into the old place so-

and-so used to live in. They're from New York, or wherever it is they come from.' If you look different, they get even more curious. But it's not that they mean to pry or anything. But they keep an eye out for what seems different to them. Since you're both Asian, I guess most people thought you two might have something to do with Karma Cholling. You know the big Buddhist place near East Barnet."

Mei had told us about the monastery and how Buddhism was growing in the USA, so I was not surprised. But I told the farmer that we didn't have any connection; that we weren't even Buddhist but Christian. He asked how that came to be; if we were converted when we came to the USA. We stood for some time, explaining and chatting. We knew that part of the information we gave him would also enter the conversation of others in the town who asked about us, the two Asians who moved into Pingsbrooke.

There is only a thin line between local and parochial; between small town and small-minded. For while some praise small towns, others, like Sinclair Lewis in *Main Street*, have condemned their stagnation and closed-mindedness. Many born in such towns have left for big cities and wider horizons – especially since the 1930s. So in today's America, the small town has a double image. It is both the society that many would wish to return to for a sense of community and belonging. Yet it is also the place others deride as being too provincial and old-fashioned.

This attitude seems at once both sentimental and condescending. But whether liked or disliked, the small town talk today focuses more on survival. As money, jobs and people flow to the big cities and nodes in an increasingly globalised world, the small town may become extinct. That possibility saddens. For small towns like Saint Johnsbury still have something to teach Americans as a residue of what they have left and lost – both good and bad. For us Singaporeans, such places say something to those who believe all Americans are more sophisticated than we are and those who say this country has no sense of community.

We settled into the routine of life. We woke at dawn with the sun, when the valley was full of mist. After a warm drink and washing up, we went to work. Jin Hua headed off to Mei's study, a small building next to the house with just a desk and some books, far enough to focus on her Master's thesis. I too was writing; stories at a desk in the loft bedroom, looking out over the valley, at the mountains. By noon, we had worked for about five hours and were ready for lunch, which we took turns making. When the weather was good and leaves turned to fall colours of red and gold, we would make a picnic and go out for an afternoon walk through the hills. Other afternoons, when the weather turned colder, were for reading by the large, bright windows, by the wood-burning stove.

Returning to Pingsbrooke by early evening, we would pick vegetables fresh from the garden. Then back in the well-stocked country kitchen, we would make dinner and linger over the large helpings and wine. By ten, sometimes even earlier, we would lock up, put out the gas-lamps and go to bed. It was a quiet routine, far easier than in the city. Our lives there took on much of that rich quietude and simplicity.

VERMONT SNAPSHOT (I) We were singing songs from the 1960s in a parlour lit by candles, fuelled by champagne and Peter's guitar. Past midnight – late by country standards – our voices went up into the cool summer sky. That was how we came to know Dave and Mary Anne. They were not Vermont natives; they summered there. And that was when we met them during our short summer visit, at a party in their Victorian country house, half-redone and barely furnished. Some years ago, they had come to visit Pingsbrooke and loved it so much they decided to buy a house nearby. They enjoyed the summer so much that, when we returned to Pingsbrooke, they were still lingering, putting off their return to their home in Toronto.

We met for dinner. Mary Anne drew us a rough map of the rural backroads. Dave let us know that he would come back to Vermont on his own for a few weeks, to work on a book of history that he was trying to finish. He promised to come by again to show us around.

It was an unusually warm September afternoon when Dave drove up to the house in his golden Japanese jeep. He couldn't believe it: as warm as summer. He said this over and over, as if the weather was a confirmation of his decision to come back. Then we went to Harvey's pond, a nearby lake. In the summer, the small beach on one end was crowded and boats sped along the calm surface on the other side. But that September afternoon, we had the place almost all to ourselves. The water was clean and calm, almost perfectly reflecting the hill slopes, the lakeside houses and the leaves – just beginning to change colour. The water was also cold despite the heat of the day. I swam for perhaps 15 minutes. Then I sat next to Jin on the soft grass, and warmed myself in the unseasonably strong sun. Dave, more accustomed to the cold, swam on until it was nearly evening. When he came out, he was sniffling a little but still talking about the gorgeous day. Then we went to eat in the town's new Chinese restaurant.

The restaurant was authentic insofar as the staff and cook were Chinese. They spoke Mandarin and Hokkien and at first I tried the little I had picked up at Harvard. Their English was rough but comprehensible after half a dozen years in America; better, at any rate, than my Chinese. Their food was equally translated: dishes like mu-gu-gai-pan and chop suey told us they were more American-Chinese than Asian-Chinese. Dave did not know better. He dug into the mu-gu-gai-pan, surprised to learn that the dish was not served in Asia. We talked about America.

Dave used to teach at the Massachusetts Institute of Technology; then he worked with the Smithsonian Institute. Both are renowned, part of the best America offers to the world. But he left both places unhappily. At MIT, he complained that a blinkered, pro-establishment atmosphere black-listed him for his political views. The Smithsonian, Dave said, blocked his planned exhibition on the Luddite movement, which was against technology, and forced him to resign. The idea that American institutions might do such things surprised me. I asked about radical intellectuals like Noam Chomsky who was with MIT. Chomsky had publicly criticised the American government as an imperial power and the press of being its collaborator: surely, his presence at MIT demonstrated that American institutions were free of political constraints? Dave squinted at us, smiled and launched into his reply, at once both persuasively intelligent and belligerent.

"You can't get rid of Chomsky. You have to understand that. He's won the Nobel Prize, for Chrissakes. Others who aren't that famous, that's a different question. And even Chomsky gets marginalised because of his views. The newspapers don't cover him. You hardly ever see him on TV. Sure, he's published but by which magazines? Small independents with a limited circulation, not the big guys. They try to ignore him. All you see on TV or read in the papers are the same guys, with more or less the same points of view. Intellectuals in America are ignored. Real intellectuals, I mean, those who question the whole basis of the system. Not just guys who want to sell some new policy to the government.

"You should meet this guy I know. He's probably written more about intellectuals in America than anyone else. He can't even get a job in a university. Hundreds of mediocre PhDs get hired, and this guy gets by-passed all the time. If it's not a conspiracy, it still shows that all these so-called 'independent' universities think in about the same way. They don't want people with different ideas, people who might make trouble.

"I made up my mind before, but I left for Canada during the Gulf War. That was really it for me, you know.

Everyone was talking about America as if it really cared about good and bad, small and big nations. It was just about the oil, goddammit. We should have admitted it. But no one wanted to hear it. You couldn't get on TV or in the press with those kinds of views. Everyone wanted to talk about what a just and clean war that was. That's how it is. The mainstream decides what it wants to hear, and what it doesn't want to know.

"I'll give you an example. I was on a TV programme recently. They wanted to talk about globalisation and technology. They had this guy who was laid off from an engineering job in his home town because the whole firm went bust. Then, he was hired by a firm that was thousands of miles away. He now 'tele-commutes' to work. That is, most days, he communicates with his colleagues through the computer, or even by video-conferencing. He travels only once a month or so. So the TV producer thinks this is a miracle of technology. The other guests on the programme are all enthusiastic about globalisation and the possibilities of working from home while interacting with people thousands of miles away.

"Me? I wanted to ask them why the old firm in the man's hometown closed down in the first place. It was globalisation too, you see. The technology made it possible for the bigger engineering firm to compete across a wider geographical area. So it out-performed the old firm. All over the world, small local companies are being wiped out by bigger ones because of the globalisation process. As far as I saw it, the technology that everyone else was so wild about was only giving the guy back the job that it had taken from him. Who knows how many others from the old firm got laid off and were never offered a chance for a second job?

"I tried to say that on the TV programme but the producer almost had a fit. He couldn't see my point or maybe he didn't want to. At the end, when they asked all of us for our last comments, I managed to sneak in what I thought people should do about technology. Fight back, that was my solution. Sabotage: that's what I said. Like the Luddites. Sabotage! You should have seen their faces."

He laughed, loud and long. But his eyes stared out, without humour. The laughter stopped abruptly. He ate his mu-gu-gai-pan with relish. He talked on about radical American intellectuals. It was familiar enough after a year of university-town discussions, yet seemed odd here. It seemed a fragment of New York or Cambridge, springing from a wholly different mind-set, too cosmopolitan for a rural setting. Dave, fired up, did not notice or care. When the topic was eventually exhausted, he launched into another tale about America. This one was about Christianity and the religious right. He went on through the rest of the meal, all through the drive back to Pingsbrooke. Once there, he carried on for a while more while we sat on the porch of the house, under the stars.

I felt tired, distant after the afternoon's activity. Or perhaps it was the reaction to the MSG in the mediocre Chinese food. Dave's stories and theories were interesting. But, sitting on the porch of the house, something in me longed for just the quiet darkness of the Vermont night. Despite all the years of city life in Singapore, quiet was something which I quickly grew addicted to. Perhaps he felt the same way, or else he was tired, but finally Dave too lapsed into silence. Then he drove home. We saw him off. We could follow his departure from the headlights of his car, blazing bright in the darkness, seen intermittently between the dark trees, on the winding road that led away from Pingsbrooke. The hard sound of the engine echoed in the hills. It was a cool evening. The unseasonal heat had dissipated and, although there would be many sunny days to come, we would never be able to go swimming again. We stood there, in front of the house on the hill, waiting for the last sound of Dave's car engine to fade into the distance. And as our eyes adjusted to the dark, after the headlights, we looked up and the Vermont sky, unobscured by clouds, was full of silent stars.

COMMUNITY   From the hill at Pingsbrooke, you looked out into a valley, across the land. There was a good view of the Green Mountains far away and, even further, you could see New York state. But you could not see your neighbours. The main road was far away, bending back behind the farm, and did not pass your view. When night came, there was no light to be seen from a street or another house, just the stars and the moon. Sometimes a car passed on the dirt road, its engine echoing in the hills. Most other times, we could only hear the wind and the occasional howl of a wild dog.

Nothing in our work and what we did connected us to the community around us. If we had stayed at Pingsbrooke, we might have believed we were the only people alive. When we had arrived, we prepared for this life of splendid isolation and work. We thought we would not get to know anyone in the few short months of fall. Mei and Peter had left the house to us with both the promise of quiet and a shotgun in the closet in case of disturbance. "Really, it's a safe community," Mei assured us. "But there are wild animals – coyotes – and thieves may come if they think the house is empty. But you can't count on the police. They're too few and too far away."

So, in this quiet but unguarded world, car lights in the driveway startled us. I looked at my watch. It was almost 10.30 at night, late by countryside standards. Who was it? What did they want? The car lights dazzled in the darkness of everything else. The idle of the engine was loud against the silence. I went out and stood on the back porch. In some part of my mind, I wondered if I should get the shotgun.

"It's me, Minty!" the driver called from the car. Minty was our nearest neighbour, an accountant and mother of three. Her voice was strained. She got out the car and, standing in the car headlights, I could see she looked anxious. I walked down from our porch. She greeted me, apologised for the late hour and asked her pressing question: "Have you seen our dog?"

The neighbours who lived closest to Pingsbrooke were the Conants: Minty Conant and her husband, Dave, their children and black-and-white dog – now missing. Dave was a botanist who taught at the nearby state college. Minty worked from home, doing the accounts of different small companies in town. We passed their house when we drove out to town or went for a walk. On mornings and weekends, we saw Dave astride the old tractor, working the hilly land around his low, sprawling house. In the evenings one of the Conant girls would be out riding their horse. If we passed when no one was at home, their dog would invite himself and join us for a walk. If the Conants were in, there was a friendly wave or a chat about the happenings in town.

From them, we learnt about where to fix the Honda good and cheap when the stones of the dirt roads kicked a hole into our exhaust. We heard about the deer that walked across the path just outside Pingsbrooke in the night and early morning. Dave suggested one or two walks in the hills nearby. We also found out about the beginning of the hunting season, when it would no longer be safe to walk in the woods because of the hunters. This accretion of small conversations, of helpful suggestions and information, would mount in the following months. It became more than most neighbours in Singapore would say to each other in a year. Partly, this was because Jin and I knew so little of Vermont and its customs. Maybe it was because the Conants were particularly friendly people. But more, there was something in the countryside that brought out a sense of friendliness and community.

Seclusion in a small town is not easy. Unless you are chilly or refuse to wave when you walk past on the country roads, when you've been into a shop two or three times and people greet you, you start talking. Some will tell you their entire life story given half a chance; others will tell you about good places for fishing or invite you to drop by their house, any time. Despite all the reported fears about crime, many Americans remain open and hospitable, particularly outside the big cities. So when we moved into our friends' house in the country, we inherited their neighbours.

They were not inquisitive or intrusive, respecting the fences and distance that you could put between yourself and the rest of the world in a rural community. But they were not as distant as physical space suggested. They did not pry or intrude on you – there was more than enough physical space to separate people – nor were they likely to offer you a life-long friendship. But in all our encounters, we found that many were open and welcoming. And now here was Minty, our inherited neighbour, standing on our porch in the middle of the night, frantic over her missing dog, Victor.

I told Minty we had seen him earlier that day on our afternoon walk past their place, and he had followed us for a while. But he had left us and, we presumed, had gone back on his own. She said there was a pack of wild dogs in the area, maybe coyotes. She was worried they had either attacked him or got him to join them. She asked us to let her know if we saw him the next day. We said we would. And then Minty got back into her car and drove off. After a while, we decided to head out ourselves, in our car, to look for Victor. There was a spot he sometimes went to at Pingsbrooke and maybe he was there. He was not, and we called Minty to tell her that. But somehow it felt right to be out there, in the night, looking for a dog. It seemed like something neighbours would do for each other.

Another native of Barnet we came to know was Marvin Bailey. He drove the local school bus and, while Mei and Peter lived at Pingsbrooke all year round, ferried their daughter, Marian, to school each morning. Marvin, in his 70s, was a tall, lanky figure almost always wearing blue denim dungarees. He was born and had always lived around Barnet, "in these here parts". He certainly was in evidence. When we asked for locally-made maple syrup, rather than the type you buy in supermarkets, someone suggested buying it from Marvin. Not only a bus driver, he made syrup by tapping the sap from the trees – much as rubber trees are tapped – and boiling that down in huge vats.

When we went to the farmer's market, Marvin was also there. He sold not just syrup but also the peas, tomatoes, pumpkins and squash that he grew. When the town's historical society put on an exhibition for the fall festival, Marvin was there explaining photos and memorabilia of bygone days. His stories, told in an accent that could not be imitated, were the oral history of the community.

"I've lived here all my life. I remember when horses pulled the snow ploughs. Most of Barnet was being re-built after the big flood. Fairfax Scales was a booming business, you see, their weighing machines were the market leaders and they had a big factory just in Saint Johnsbury. I didn't want to go anywhere else. I didn't think to, I suppose I never felt the urge. I've been to Boston a few times but it wasn't for me. No, not for me."

Marvin's choice was clear. He preferred to keep on tapping maple syrup, working his small farm and selling the produce at the farmer's market on weekends and to continue driving the school bus so long as his eyesight was good. Instead of a cosmopolitan city, he chose to remain in the area, with the places and the community he knew and had grown up in.

Community was a resurgent theme in America. President Clinton had spoken much about community and responsibility, both in his first presidential campaign and since. That theme was amplified in inner cities where the lack of jobs and breakdown of families had added to violence and areas in which people feared the street rather than greeted their neighbour. It was taken up by academics who spoke of "communitarianism": balancing individual rights with community responsibility.

In the town, however, communitarianism might be unheard of. It was simply understood among people like Marvin. People who worked for, sold to, bought from and knew their community. A town where you knew most people who walked down the street, at least by face if not by name. Perhaps only those who no longer have a community talk about it.

Still, the communitarian message may help a new generation in such towns maintain what they already have. For, with changes in the economy and people moving in and out, younger Americans are much less likely to be as rooted and part of their community as Marvin Bailey. This change was exemplified by an event related to Dave and Minty's missing dog.

Three days later I walked on the country road past the Conants' house. Dave was on the porch. When he saw me, he waved and came up to tell me they had found Victor. The dog had wandered off with the child of a family that lived two miles down the road. After it was there for a few hours and wouldn't leave their property, they called for the town's dog catcher. He came, got the dog and – since it had a tag – gave him to the vet. The vet called Dave and Minty and, after three days and a $70 fee, their dog was home. But it was not an entirely happy ending.

"I don't understand why they didn't just call me and not the dog catcher," Dave said, shaking his head. "They just moved in last year. But we're neighbours and they should know." Dave looked across, quizzically, seeming to seek reassurance, even if I was the newest person to move into the area. Yes, I wanted to say. That was what they should have done. After all they were part of the community, I wanted to add. But perhaps they weren't.

VERMONT SNAPSHOT (II) Frank was another neighbour in the hills around Pingsbrooke. He came up the drive in his old pick-up late one morning while I was boiling water in the kitchen. I stood on the porch as he got out, and Jin soon joined us. He was a stout man, with a grey moustache and beard, dressed in denim jacket and jeans with a checked work shirt.

"Hi," he greeted me, friendly, as if we already knew each other.

"Hello," I said back.

"Heard you were living here now. And I wondered if Mei was around too. If she is," he continued as he walked up, "I was hoping we could meditate together. I'm Frank."

Mei was a Buddhist. There was a large Buddhist sanctuary near the farm. Many of the town people had assumed that, as Asians, we too were Buddhists. Some assumed we were related to Mei; her sister had stayed on the farm some time ago but she didn't like it and had moved out. That was what Frank asked us too, when I told him Mei was not with us. Were we relatives and Buddhists?

He seemed disappointed, perhaps a little mystified to learn that we were not. What more that we were Christians. It was as if they – White, blonde Westerners – and we – dark-haired Asians – had been moving in opposite directions in religion. We would not meditate with Frank. "But come in for some tea," I invited him, and he did.

Frank had not always been a Buddhist. He was born into a church-going family in a small town. He had first stepped outside the mainstream by becoming a musician. He used to play with Ray Charles, he told us. He had travelled through most of North and South America as a musician, a sideman. He used to do drugs. Then he became a Buddhist. Buddhism was enjoying a renaissance in America. It was seen as something outside the mainstream, associated with Beat poets like the famous Dharma bum, Jack Kerouac. Almost all the followers at the monastery in Vermont were like Frank, White Americans who had come to Buddhism late in life, as a matter of conscious choice, sometimes as a rejection of the middle-class Christianity that marked their earlier life.

"I didn't stop drugs entirely," Frank told us. "But I laid off the heavy stuff. I got a grip on it. Discipline, that's what Buddhism gave me, discipline and a new way of thinking about things. After a while, I gave up the road. I knew it was bad for me, all that travelling. It was too lonely for me. So I settled down here, got married."

Frank built a large, pagoda-like house, the only one of its kind in the state. But he was now going through a messy divorce. He might be ejected from the pagoda house and had already lost his sense of equanimity. Hence, his request for us to join him in meditation. But we had tea together and talked. He spoke openly about his problems. Most Americans like to tell people about their lives. But Frank spoke in a way that was different from the normal gregariousness, as if he had been lonely and silent for too long. We listened and poured tea.

The only time he seemed less sad was when he talked about playing music. After an hour or so, Frank left, with a wave of his arm and a sad but friendly smile. We told him that Mei would come up sometime in the fall and we would tell her he had come by. He spoke warmly of Mei and invited us to visit him whenever we wanted, before he had to move out of the pagoda house.

A few days later, a pick-up came up the drive again. When I first went out, I thought it would be Frank. But it was a different pick-up with a different man in it. "Hi," he called from the driver's seat, "I'm Virgil. I was wondering if you'd seen a dog?"

I laughed and then explained how the Conants had come looking for their dog too. It tempted me to ask if they came to us because someone had heard Chinese ate dogs. But the Conants had been earnest in their concern. And, as for Virgil, he seemed less worried that we had harmed the dog than that the dog would harm us.

"If you see my dog, don't go near him," he warned. "He's kinda a wolf dog. Had him bred special, strong and brave but a little wild. There's been a pack of wild dogs or wolves around the place and each night they were howling and acting up, and I could see my dog listening and wanting to join them. It was as if he was becoming a wild dog too. So if you see him – he's yellow and big – don't go near him or anything. Just call me, and let me know where you saw him."

Virgil got out of the pick-up while we were talking. He was a tall, large-boned man with straggly long hair and an unkempt beard. He wore a denim shirt and worn, grungy corduroy jeans. There was something in his look and especially in his wide eyes, like he was a bit of a wild dog himself. Virgil talked on about the area and the people around us. Who lived where, who hunted deer and where. There was a divide between the community. There were those, like Virgil, who had been around a long time, who knew the land well and hunted deer in season. And there were others who were old hippies and refugees from the city. They did not hunt. Virgil did not name these non-hunters, but it was clear that Mei was one of them.

We walked around the house a while. Virgil had a way of telling stories. He had been an expert in insulation systems and worked for a computer company in Boston for a few years. He had two girls, a wife and an ex-wife, and a holiday house in Miami. One of our neighbours was having an affair with a woman from a nearby town; this one was on the verge of divorce (that was Frank, I supposed); the other was thought to be going a little crazy. As we walked and talked, Virgil kept spitting, a dirty brown spittle: chewed tobacco. He offered me some but I declined. A bit more than an hour passed and, by the end, I knew a bit about the land around us and about deer hunting, and a lot of the local gossip.

A few weeks later, Peter called us. They would have a few days off from work at the college over the holidays and thought of coming up to Pingsbrooke. We looked forward to seeing them. Just because we were there didn't mean that it wasn't still their home.

"How are you two settling in?" Peter asked kindly. "Have you met anyone?" I told him about Frank and Virgil, their two friends who came by. Or rather, I mentioned them. It was Peter who told me about them.

"Virgil . . . Virgil . . . Is he the guy who lives in a trailer at the end of the road? Tall, with dirty yellow hair, chews tobacco? If that's him, we don't know him well at all. Be careful with him. He's lived in that house even when it almost fell down around his ears. He just trashed the place. Then, rather than fixing it up, he just got a trailer. Can you believe that?

"As for Frank, he's not really a close friend. I mean he's a Buddhist but I don't think he's ever meditated with Mei. He probably came round because he was feeling bad about his divorce. He's never come up to the house before. I mean, I feel sorry for him . . . divorce can't be easy. But don't feel obliged to be nice to him or anything."

I listened carefully to Peter. He was a good man, with fair judgment and honesty, on top of a sense of humour. He was not telling us to isolate these people. He was simply making sure we knew what they were like; that we would not extend ourselves to people like Frank and Virgil under the mistaken impression they were their friends, or because we thought that was the thing to do in a country community. He steered us towards the Conants if we needed help or just someone to talk to. He named one or two other people in the area who Mei and he had really come to know well and trust.

We didn't go out to meet Frank or Virgil. And they never turned up at the farm again. Maybe they knew what Peter or his friends must have told us about them. Or perhaps, having talked to us, they realised they didn't want to be our friends; thought us a strange, foreign couple. It would not have surprised me. A small community, I realised, is not a place where everyone gets on with everyone else, as if they are part of some extended, happy family. No, some are friends, people you get on with, and others are not. A small community simply means you know people and learn to make judgments about them.

Another thing that a small community forces on you is self-reliance. It is not just making do with fewer people around. There are daily things that are taken for granted in city life. Out in the countryside, in Vermont, we put up with a lot of rubbish. Not that life was unpleasant. The rubbish was literal. In Cambridge, rubbish was collected once a week. A blue plastic bin sat on a city sidewalk, next to the rubbish, for newspapers, glass bottles, tin cans, paper and plastic bags: all these and more were set aside and taken away for recycling. Recycling in many America urban centres is quite widespread, easy and efficient. It is also based on economics. Deposits give people incentives to return and recycle. When they don't, the jobless and homeless often collect cans off the street to return for extra change. For aluminium cans and other items with deposits major supermarkets provide collection centres which look like vending machines. When the can is put into the slot, the machine gives you a slip to exchange for cash.

It didn't work the same way in Vermont. Out in the countryside, houses were so widely spread out that the garbage was not collected by the municipal garbage truck. Rather, each household took its own garbage to the town dump and paid for disposal.

From Pingsbrooke, the nearest place was in Passumpsic. The dump was only open on Saturdays, from nine to noon. The charge was $1.50 per bag. So it became part of our ritual, a fixed appointment in our otherwise elastic weekly calendar of life there. Each week, we would tie up the big black rubbish bins, line the car boot with plastic and drive down to the dump. Fortunately, in the cool, the rubbish did not smell bad and the farm had a compost heap which turned most organic and vegetable waste into natural fertiliser. Still, there was an initial, squeamish reaction to handling the rubbish and putting it into the car. But that was part of the self-reliance that life in the countryside taught us. Others around us, used to it, made the effort without thinking twice.

Recycling required even more effort. The town had only one recycling centre, volunteer-run and open just once a month in a school carpark. We had to drive ten miles with our bottles and things. There – rain or shine, sun or snow – the volunteers sorted out things that could not be taken (like oil containers). For the recyclable items, they stripped labels off bottles and flattened tin cans. The effort by these volunteers explained why we had to pay them, rather than the reverse. In the countryside, if you believed in recycling, you put money and effort into it.

Electricity was another convenience that Pingsbrooke did not have. At least not the kind you got simply by flicking on a switch, day or night. The farmhouse was wired up with gas and the lights worked like hurricane camping lamps, with a thin veil of white wire holding the lit gas like a bulb. That served for general lighting, although it was too dim for reading or other close work. But electricity was still needed for other uses, appliances like the washing machine and the water pump. The farm was not supplied by electricity cables, like the houses in Saint Johnsbury and houses nearer the road. For that, there was a gas-run generator. It came on easily enough, with a flick of a switch, but it made a rumble and ran only so long as there was enough gas in the tank. I had to keep it fuelled up and make sure its oil was changed.

The generator allowed the house to be on its own, further away from the road. The inconvenience seemed a small price to pay for privacy. Once in a while, it would also fail to start when we switched it on. I would then go out to check its battery or start it with the starter rope. This chore was easy enough when the weather was good. But when it was cold and the wind was whipping, I missed the convenience of city-supplied electricity.

Manual work became a natural part of our days at Pingsbrooke. Jin enjoyed the garden. She reaped the harvest of organic vegetables and made sure our table was always well supplied with the sun-ripened tomatoes, zucchini and other fresh produce. When frost came on clear nights in September and October, it was Jin who rallied us to cover the patch with large plastic sheets, to save the vegetables from freezing. As for me, I specialised in keeping the wood stoves going. The gas heaters were sufficient to keep the house warm, but the wood – taken from fallen or replanted trees – was plentiful and cheaper. The stoves also completed the country atmosphere at the farm.

This meant that I learnt to wield the two axes in the wood shed. One was broad and blunt, meant for cutting the bigger logs. The second was finer, for chopping them thin to kindle the fire. It was fairly hard work, enough to build up some sweat even when the ground was frosty in the morning. I would chop wood three times a day: in the morning to get the house warm; then in the afternoon, to keep the fire going slowly; and again before nightfall, a large load, to keep us warm through the night. The task appealed to me as a break from the writing at my desk. It gave me an excuse to be outdoors for a spell. It was a challenge to break the wood with a few strokes of the axe. A mix of simple physical exertion and concentration was required. And when I was chopping wood, I felt a mental keenness that refreshed me for writing.

The wood shed was off to the side of the house and looked down the hill. On some days, I would be chopping wood at sunset. If the writing had gone well during the day, and we had walked during the afternoon, there was nothing more complicated to look forward to in the evening but an hour of cooking what we liked and then more time to eat it, lingering over food and wine and talking, then washing up, putting out the rubbish and taking a slow walk to dump the vegetable cuttings at the compost heap near the vegetable garden. We would then return to the house under the clear night sky with the stars and moon out for an early night.

On such evenings, despite a lifetime of living in the city and of being surrounded by people, I missed no one. I did not miss the conveniences of electricity and other urban services. And the darkness and isolation did not scare us, even when the wind blew strong over the hills and a wild dog or wolf howled somewhere in the distance.

THE BEST LITTLE TOWN The "Business District" sign was prominent in Littleton but there were just two blocks of shops and offices, between a church with a tall spire and a bank. Walking along the main street, at noon on a weekday, there were no crowds to jostle you. The traffic was light except for an occasional long-haul truck; there were pedestrian crossings and four-way "stop" signs rather than traffic lights. From "opening sale" and "new management" signs, there were at least four new shops and businesses, although several shop spaces remained vacant. Economic growth was perceptible on Main Street, USA, but not booming. In one unit, posters, pictures and text made up a mini-exhibition to explain why people should set up business here. This was topped by the large sign "The best little town in America".

The accolade was self-awarded. I had come across many other places in the country where the locals felt they had found the best place to be. It was part of the self-pride and self-promotion that churned American social and economic life. But, as I stood on the pavement outside the exhibition, something in me acknowledged that what I had seen of this town was pleasant. The streets were clean, so was the air. Parking was easy enough. There were cheery and helpful people in the bicycle shop and in the diner near the corner, which served a good pancake breakfast, washed down with thin brown-water coffee. On the street, people said hello in passing a neighbour. There was a sense of activity, without the hustle and bustle of a larger place. It seemed nice, like other small towns spread across the continent.

I went into an overcrowded bookstore. Dusty shelves were weighed down by new and used books, arranged by subjects such as fiction, music and how-to-do. The bookstore owner was a tall man in his 50s, with white hair and no glasses. He wore a simple pair of corduroys and a white shirt. I asked him about the town. He told me about the way things had been in this town when he was young, about the way things were better under Reagan, when America was number one. He called President Clinton a liberal, using the word as if it were a term of abuse. He steered me to a rack of books that was prominently displayed. "If you want to know what is happening in the real America, read these books," he said proudly.

I scanned the shelves. There were tracts by Pat Buchanan who, in early 1992 campaigns, upstaged then President George Bush with strong support from the religious Right. The writings of radio host Rush Limbaugh stood alongside more academic books, such as Alan Bloom's *The Closing of the American Mind*. At the top of the book rack, a sign read "Conservatism".

American conservatism is pro-community, pro-family and values, pro-business, pro-military and pro-church. It is also anti-taxes, anti-big government, anti-affirmative action, anti-abortion and anti-welfare. In the 1990s, conservatism has been associated with moves to restrict the number of immigrants from Latin America, Asia and other non-European countries.

Conservatism is generally pro-Republican, although some Republicans are more liberal and some democrats more conservative. It is clearly anti-Clinton. After Clinton's election, some thought conservatism would decline, having peaked during the Reagan years. But, almost from the first initiative of his administration to allow gays in the military, President Clinton had become a focus of the conservatives' attack.

I looked at the bookstore owner. He was a garrulous man with a hard, clipped way of speaking. He talked on about how things used to be, and how the country needed to be put right. He used "we" when he spoke. I did not know if the word referred to a conservative association he might belong to, like the American legion, or his church, or if he simply identified his thought with those of a broad but unnamed community. When I asked, he was affronted.

"The average American, that's who I mean. I know what some others may say – especially in those big city newspapers. But this is what we think, what we've always thought. It's only now that we've had the chance to be heard. Do you know how many people listen to Rush Limbaugh now? Well, those people weren't born yesterday, I can tell you. They were just waiting for someone to speak up on all the things they've always been thinking. Not those liberals and what have you, but average Americans, real Americans like us."

He steered me back to the rack of books, naming some titles and giving me a run-down of what they said. He went on for a while like this, part political demagogue, part salesman. I was surprised that he was so forthright when, by my skin, he could tell that I was not an "average" American. How did he know I would not be offended by his political opinions? Perhaps he did not care; that was his way of telling me I was welcome to visit, but not to stay in the town. Or maybe he simply did not care what I thought because he was sure he was right. Perhaps he was, at least in one respect. Many Americans like him and many small towns like this one may always have been conservative. The only change was that that strand had become more visible and vocal since the 1980s.

Then another customer came into the shop, a regular, and he excused himself. I heard them talking about a town meeting and the upcoming state elections. In the state elections that the bookstore owner and his friends were discussing, "liberal" had become a dirty label. One candidate condemned his rival for being "Bill Clinton's best friend". In the 1994 election, an association with the incumbent president of the USA was a liability rather than an asset. I browsed for a while longer, then excused myself without buying anything. The bookstore owner looked up briefly, but said nothing.

When I went out, I found that conservatism had grown beyond this bookstore and its owner. It ran out the store and along the street. A block down, Cheryl ran a business selling artwork and frames. Small and blonde, the mother of two came to this small town from New York some 17 years ago. "I marched in anti-Vietnam demonstrations and all those sort of things in the 1970s," she explained. "I guess I was a liberal. But then I started teaching. There was so much drugs and violence. Many of the kids had no fathers, you know. Some could curse worse than anything I knew – and they were just six or seven." Then 20-something, she taught in inner-city schools. In two years, Cheryl the liberal became exhausted and disillusioned. "I wanted my sons to grow up in a better environment. That's one of the big reasons we came out here."

In her shop, there were lines on a pillar marked at different heights, with the names Sam and Peter written next to each. "Yes," Cheryl laughed when I pointed them out, "that's where I measured my sons as they grew."

Cheryl was not anti-abortion or anti-welfare. Nor was she a member of a church. She had never read books from the bookstore's shelf of conservatism titles. She did not know the owner well, she said. But she too emphasised family, community and the need for America to do something. Experience had changed her from the liberal she was. She was a liberal who had been mugged by reality – to use a phrase coined by arch-conservative commentator Irving Kristol. Her conversion was part of what has been called the conservative revolution. Conservatism – old and new, both the bookstore owner and Cheryl – stood against many if not all the things that liberalism brought in the 1960s. The liberal, the hippie, the radical and the permissive were no longer prevalent in America. Socially, politically, such icons were out of fashion. Perhaps, in small towns like Littleton, they would always have been. With conservatism, a different American was emerging, or perhaps re-emerging. It was an American who emphasised family, business and other values. And with this, there may be less difference in social attitudes between America and Asia than some imagined.

Standing in the main street of the town, I wondered, however, if they could see that similarity. There were no other Asians in town as far as we could tell. Nor were there many African-Americans or other minorities. The town, the whole state, seemed 99 per cent White American. That would have an impact on the face and shade of skin the conservatives in the town imagined when they pictured the "average" American. I looked up at the steeple of the church and across to the end of the business district. Perhaps this was the best little town in America. Perhaps it was, like many other towns across the country, conservative at its core. It all seemed pleasant and agreeable enough. But as Jin Hua and I got into our little red Japanese car, I saw ourselves reflected in the window of an empty store front, a few down from the bookstore and art gallery. The colour of our foreign car and of our Asian skin was apparent. We were different, and that difference transcended the fact that we were only visitors, not members of this community. The tidy Main Street could not transform itself into the vastly different landscapes of ghettos, skyscrapers, Hollywood and Silicon Valley arrayed across America. Nor did it seem that the core beliefs of this conservative town could accommodate America's many different constituencies – those from urban and metropolitan communities, whether sophisticated or poor, and those from ethnic or religious minorities. We drove out of town, glad to have visited but also glad not to be staying.

LEAVING PINGSBROOKE The colours of fall faded and its leaves crumpled. One night, the wind blew hard and long through the hills. And the next morning, we awoke to a landscape of bare trees, thin and black branches, ready for winter. Days remained sunny and there was still some beauty in the piles of fallen leaves. But the temperatures had dropped and the landscape turned bleak. It was hunting season. Through the day, the silence of the hills would break and echo with gunfire. We put an end to our walks. Not just because of the colder weather; the Conants and everyone whom we had met in those short months warned us to stay out of the woods during hunting season. Our movements might otherwise be mistaken by a hunter for deer, and we would be summarily shot.

The vegetable garden that had fed us so well through the fall months was nearly bare. One afternoon, after a spate of night frosts, we took in what remained of the vegetables. We cut off the huge sunflower blooms that had grown too heavy for their weakening stalks. Back at the house, we dried them – first on the wooden porch in the sun and then in the oven. Then we beat the sunflower heads and roasted the seeds with some salt. The root vegetables that could survive the winter – radishes, turnips and potatoes – were left in the soil. At the next night frost, we left the patch uncovered. The next morning, all that remained was dead or dying, except the pumpkins, now free from their vines, huge and brilliantly orange in the green and earth-brown patch. We took them up to the house, each so large that they took us both to roll them uphill, and considerable strain to carry them down the steps into the cool, dark cellar for storage. That done, everything else, a tangle of stalks, leaves and vines, was simply left to return to the earth and increase fertility for the next year.

It was only a matter of weeks before the first snow fell. The snow on the ground reflected back the sunlight and, while we were in the house, it was even brighter than summer. At night, with the snow on the ground, the moon made the hills glow as if the earth itself was another moon. We would put out all the gas lamps and the soft and luminous light would fill the house. It was a good time to stay indoors, with work and books and a warm stove.

Going outside, however, was another matter. We had managed driving on slick city streets the previous winter in Cambridge, but the rural tracks were another matter. The ground grew soft with the snow melting.

The ruts deepened and either became slushy with water or hard with ice. Our little Civic struggled up the hills now. When the snow was deep one evening, it could not find enough traction to climb the hill, and we had to pull over and leave it for the night, and walk back. It was time to go.

The snow would thicken throughout the winter, grow icy and then, in spring, with the melt, Vermont would go into its notorious mud season. With snow and then mud, the roads that led to the farm we had come so quickly to think of as home would be near impassable, at least with our small, two-wheel-drive car and inexperience of such conditions.

We were also out of excuses to linger. Jin had finished her thesis. And for me, there were some stories and a third of a novel that I felt good about and wanted to continue later. If we could have kept things as they had been in September and October, we might have stayed permanently in Vermont. There was a simple beauty in those days that I continually relished and knew that Singapore could never emulate. But with the change of months, we knew that it was time to go. We felt that in our tropical bones, like seasonal animals.

We had never belonged in Vermont. Even if we had stayed longer and had gotten to know the area and the people better than most passers-by and travellers would, we were not natives and were not accepted as such by those who were. And this was the time to make the best of not belonging.

However, even if we recognised the facts that impelled us to go, we acted on that feeling reluctantly, out of sentiment and attachment to the house. No, to the time we had spent and the things we had learnt living there – about rural America, the community around us, ourselves and, in a way, where we had come from.

We got ready to go. We went by to the Conants to say goodbye, over a large country breakfast of pancakes and local maple syrup and fruit. We shut down the house: leaving the gas heaters at a minimum, arranging for the Conants' daughter to come by and water the plants, finishing off the food that could not be kept, replenishing the wood in the shed with extra sessions of chopping, and then locking up. Some useful things were left behind in the house – down pillows, a few books and bottles of wine. We packed the car. Less things were in it now.

We waited until the snow had almost cleared and then we went. Still, when we drove out, there was enough slick ice to get us stuck. So we stood at the side of the road, at first reluctant to leave but now, with only an empty house behind us, anxious to keep moving. Jin stayed with our car. I started walking back to the Conants to see if they were in. Otherwise, I would head back to the house to call a tow truck. It was cold and wet. We were tired from the packing and preparations to leave, and there was still a long drive ahead of us. As I trudged up the hill, it did not feel like the right way to leave a place and a time that had been so good for us.

Then I saw the truck. It was the town truck from Saint Johnsbury. In the summer, we had seen the workers prune back the overhanging branches from the trees to keep the roads clear. In the winter, it was used after the snowfall had turned to ice, for putting a layer of earth and gravel on the ice to make it easier for cars to pass. I waved the truck down and, when the driver stopped, told him about our situation.

The driver was a man in his 50s, with grey hair. He wore a ski cap and dungarees under a heavy coat. I did not know him, although I had seen him around the town sometimes – I thought at least – with Marvin Bailey, the old man who was everywhere, doing everything. He had heard of us, two Asians living out in rural Barnet. Yep, he said when he saw the red Civic, he had seen our car around the town and knew it wouldn't be much use when the snow came. It was a good time to go, he agreed, when he saw all our things packed inside.

With his help, we pushed the car out of the rut that it was stuck in. Then he got back into the truck and told us to follow him. He would lead the way out, paving the way for us with gravel and earth. And that was what we did. We went up the hill and down again, past the open field that looked out to the river and the tall stand of pine that they had been selectively cutting in the fall, and uphill again and down, finally, to the single-lane road that, because it was paved, was the local highway. The way was so familiar to us, it felt that we were just leaving for a short drive to the Green Mountains or a quick trip to the supermarket in town. But the white sprinkle of snow, the steady, rumbling truck in front of us and the carpet of earth that was laid specially for us, meant that it was a one-way trip. We were leaving.

At the end of the dirt track, where the paved road began, I tooted my horn at the truck and, as he pulled over, I pulled up alongside him. He had diverted from his route to help us. I thanked him and, in addition, offered him a sum of money. There was no need, he said, it was just his job. I offered him the money again, and again he refused. He was just pleased he could help. I thanked him and got back into our car. We waved and we drove away. A man who didn't know us, to whom we were aliens in a foreign-made car, had helped us for no reason other than it was partly his job and partly the pleasure of helping someone. I drove away from Pingsbrooke, from Barnet and Passumpsic and Saint Johnsbury, and out of the state of Vermont.

There were still weeks ahead of us in America. Returning to Cambridge, we would stay with Ken and Danna to catch up and also do practical things like submitting Jin Hua's thesis and arranging for our books and things to be shipped home; I would go to Philadelphia to give a talk at the college where Mei taught, and Washington to visit a family friend; we would holiday in the south, where it was still warm. That was all still ahead of us, before we would get onto the plane for Singapore, and there were moments we enjoyed and in which we learnt more about the country and its people. But I knew, from the moment I left that man and his truck by that road in Vermont, that there would be no better way to leave America.

concluding
a continent

heading
home

HOME is a place in which you feel comfortable, and know all that you need to know. That, at least, is the idea the word evokes. But returning to Singapore was a return to heat and to change. The high humidity and temperature were things I had never grown completely comfortable with, even after a lifetime in Singapore. I am not alone in this, I know; the whole island is increasingly air-conditioned, in denial of our tropical climate. And after two New England winters, certainly, I had no endurance for it.

The changes in Singapore were equally uncomfortable. Less than two years had passed since we had left. It was not a long time. In Cambridge, walking around the Square before we left, the shops were much the same as when we arrived. Staff at the Harvard Book Store remembered me and cheerfully filled my final order of books, almost twenty kilograms worth, at a special discount. Harvie was hanging around with his latest issue of *Spare Change*, still homeless but dressed warmly now for the winter. The university was in mid-session. There was a new class, strange faces at the desks my classmates and I had filled just a year ago, but there were the same professors and the same ivy-covered buildings. In Vermont, we had seen the leaves turn from a bright leafy green to gold and red and then fall, and the snow on the ground. When the snow and mud season passed, green leaves would return to the bare winter trees, and the vegetable garden would begin to sprout again. Then, as summer's heat became fall, the fruit and vegetables would ripen and the leaves turn to their spectacular colours once more, just as we had known them. There was a rhythm to these things in Vermont, and a different time to do different things, whether it was skiing, planting, walking or hunting. But, while the seasons went through this cycle, there was little actual and permanent change, especially over two years. People spoke of winters five or even fifteen years ago as if they had just passed.

Singapore, however, had changed. New roads had been built, others re-routed. New shops and hotels had begun operation, considerable additions like the revitalised Boat Quay, Ngee Ann City, and the expansion of Marina City. Whole new housing estates, both public and private, had come up, in many cases where older, less optimal buildings had stood. Car and housing prices had risen to a level that could hardly seem possible.

Just before I left, I had written essays and captions for a book of aerial photographs, *Over Singapore*. That book helped me realise the pace of changes. Less than two years later, so much had changed that the publisher needed a new edition, with changes in photographs to show new places, and new captions to be written.

But despite these considerable changes, or perhaps because they had come so quickly and in so many ways, many Singaporeans I had met did not seem to recognise them. As I settled back in and met up with people I knew, there was little introspection about these changes. Maybe they were too busy, caught up in the rush of each day. There were few of the conversations I had known at Harvard, talking leisurely over coffee or wine about ideas, national and international issues. There was even less of the solitude and quiet neighbourliness we had experienced in Vermont. Singaporeans talked about cars and property. Knowing we had just returned from America, many also asked curiously and wistfully about our experiences.

Some envied our time away. But in the same breath that they wished they could go too, they would say it was not possible for them. They were stuck, or felt stuck, even those who were not tied down other than by jobs and mortgages as we had been. In the next breath, these people who said they wanted to go, would worry about the dangers of crime and violence in America and wonder how we had coped.

For this was another change that had happened while we were away. The debate between Singapore and the USA over systems of government and democracy had increased in the aftermath of the Michael Fay caning. It was still rising, with another controversy over the

American academic Christopher Lingle, who had written an article about Asian courts being "compliant", leading to a conviction in Singapore for contempt of court. As American criticism of Singapore had risen over the Fay and Lingle incidents, so had Singaporean replies. This was not limited to a rebuttal to specific points in these particular incidents. It spilled over into more general criticism of the USA, especially the problems of crime and the failure of American politics to deal with that issue.

America was no longer a place of promise, a country of dreams that Singaporeans looked up to and felt empathy with. It was now seen as a place of violence and danger. It was the promoter of Western attitudes that, Singaporeans were told, were incompatible with our own values. The questions that those we met put to us about the dangers in the USA reflected the tenor of many articles in the Singaporean media.

When I returned, I also realised that the columns I had written about America could be seen in a different context. For they were not what Americans would write about their own country, for either foreigners or their fellow citizens. They were articles written by a Singaporean for an audience in Singapore, by an alien Asian for others who were also alien and Asian. I had known that in part, whether I was writing from that quiet house at the dead-end road in Cambridge, in a hotel room in New York or Washington DC or the farm in Vermont. But reading the last pieces about America when I was already back in Singapore brought that feeling to me strongly.

I had kept in touch with Singapore through friends, the overseas edition of the *Straits Times* and other media. Especially when the Michael Fay incident happened, I kept a special eye on Singapore's relations with America. But, from across the Pacific, I had thought that the fundamentals of the America–Singapore relationship, built around shared security and commercial interests, would have seen them through these controversies. Until my return, I did not realise the growing intensity of the mud-slinging.

I had certainly not expected a senior American diplomat to ask, with considerable indignation and hurt, why the Singaporean media were waging an anti-American campaign. Nor did I suspect the same American to commend me on the balance of the columns I had written in that same media. As for Singaporeans, some thought I was pro-American since I had studied there on a Fulbright scholarship offered by their government, while others thought that since my columns were in the *Straits Times*, they must have been pre-approved by some censor and therefore were anti-American, subtly or otherwise. It was not, I thought, the columns themselves that had elicited those varying comments. It was the context. In the aftermath of Fay and Lingle, America remained in the headlines of the Singapore media. I had left America but America had returned with me.

But it was an America that I only partly recognised. In its transport and translation into the Singaporean context, America's image seemed distorted as if in a funny-house mirror. Some aspects were highlighted: such as crime and violence, troubled youth and families, inner-city problems and drugs, political peccadilloes and impasses. But the country's quieter and safer neighbourhoods and towns, its green and clean suburbs and communities, its stories of strength and resilience – all of which we had known during our time in the US – were less well publicised. The debate seemed in danger of providing a simplistic dichotomy, in which America was the dark place for all that Singaporeans might fear would go wrong in society. It also seemed dangerously jingoistic, with some commentators suggesting that while Asia and Singapore were on the rise, America was in rapid decline. I tried my best to present things in a more balanced way whenever I spoke to people about America.

It was with that in my mind that I wrote the last of my columns about America. I remembered the Greyhound journey I had taken, from rural Vermont down the East Coast to the capital, Washington DC, via Philadelphia and New York. I remembered how grand it felt to walk down New York's swank Fifth Avenue and linger at the Rockefeller Centre, or to see Congress and the white monuments of Washington DC, to indulge in the grandeur of the country. That was my impression when I first visited America and these sights still impressed. But a longer stay in this country, however, had made me see them differently.

Coming down the East Coast, city by city, from distant Vermont to the capital, there was a different America. The verdant hills and countryside receded into grey highways and the indifferent, even ugly, neighbourhoods on the verges of big cities. The world-class faculty and neo-classical campus of Columbia University in New

York straddled streets ruled by drug kings and gangs. The Liberty Bell and Van Gogh paintings in old Philadelphia contrasted with nearby shipyards and steel towns like Bethlehem that were rusted and shut down. For each stylish and rich boulevard or university area, too many other sectors were grey, desolate. For every shiny new office building, factories elsewhere were grimy hulks. For every clear mountain stream, there was a polluted river.

These had been years of doubt for America. After the flush of celebration at the Communist collapse, America's free market democracy had faced its own problems — social, economic and political. Politicians, especially Conservative Republicans, stridently called for the return to American values and for the country to reassert itself as number one. At the street level, Americans swung between apathy and trying to "throw the bums out" in politics.

But the view on my Greyhound bus journey was more than just general moods and scenery through the window. It was worthwhile watching and talking to the people who rode with me. One of my fellow travellers was a 17-year-old African-American girl on welfare, unwed with two children. Her hair was dyed an impossible blonde, for that was what her new boyfriend wanted. Another was a cab driver, recently arrived from India, who complained loudly about Whites. There was an old man in a musty, tattered sports jacket, slumped across two seats because no one would sit next to him. There was a bright young man from a well-known business school, who spent most of his trip trying to pick up a Swedish tourist who was sitting across the aisle from him.

That was the mixture of people on the bus. For each rich and educated American, you meet many with more limited resources and expectations. For each socially committed citizen, there are others who do not care about anyone else; those who are "entertaining themselves to death" as the cultural observer, Neil Postman, put it. This small, unscientific sampling was disturbing.

A bedrock of democracy is a certain level of equality in income, education and prospects; only then can there be a community of shared interests and outlook. Instead, heightened inequalities and ethnic differences seem to be leading to what the eminent historian Schlesinger has described as the "disuniting of America". Yet the country's size and diversity maintained an immense reservoir of talent and resilience. It is too soon to write off this society as a whole or, indeed, any part of it.

"I didn't know what I was doing," a young African-American man told me as we rode the Greyhound. "I was born in the worst area. My ol' man was never around. I grew up in a gang. By the time I was 18, I'd seen stuff so bad that you wouldn't believe." Next to me, he rolled up his sleeve to show his bullet wound – a pale, dime-size mark cut through his bicep. "I was lucky it was only a flesh wound. Then I found God and some self-respect." He told me he worked in an express delivery service. In his free time, he helped at a half-way house for street children. He was thinking of becoming a preacher and began to tell me about his conversion.

Immigrants can tell a similar story. On another leg of my journey, I met a woman from Honduras who had lived in New York for ten years and was running a small clothing manufacturer. "It's tougher these days," she admitted. "The danger of living in the city, the poor economy, these sort of things make me think of going home. But I did last summer," she told me candidly, "and I decided to come back. The opportunities in America are better." Despite its present problems, opportunities in this country continue to attract immigrants. And the promise of democracy is part of the continuing attraction.

These people were examples of a better America. For many – new immigrants like the Honduran woman or those born poor, like the would-be preacher – it is still a land of opportunities and second chances. For some who are united and active, like the group of Asian-Americans I met at Swarthmore, democracy here can still be made to work – especially at a local level where the community is small enough for different voices to be heard. Where democracy does work, those who practise it feel part of the country. There seemed hope for such examples. America is not a country that is rich only in money and assets. It is one that is rich in variety, experiment and possibility. It is not a country that is fixed in its ways and destiny but one that, for better and for worse, is still changing and moving forward.

I arrived in America as a student, as increasing numbers of Singaporeans do. What I came to understand was not just what I studied, but also something of this country's culture and the workings of its democracy.

These are beliefs that this superpower has transmitted around the globe. The view up-close, however, lends a different perspective. I am not one of those who still assume that all things in America are better, that their society paves the way ahead for us. This reappraisal is small. But to those who have long upheld America as a utopia and the laboratory for democracy, it is near heresy. Yet neither am I among those who think that America is in absolute decline, soon to be overtaken by Asia. The strength of a close-up view is to note not just the general but also the specific. From this perspective, despite its enormous scale, grand strengths and some-times large-scale omissions, America the superpower is not what stands out. It is instead the strength of this country's smaller communities, of nodes of excellence, and of individual Americans that can be affirmed.

From those memories and perspectives, I wrote my last article of my column "Fax From America". The only thing that remained, I thought, was to wait for the bags of books that I had mailed back. I tried to put America aside, to engage more fully with my own society. But America would still not leave me alone.

❖

Some months after I left America, Henry Steiner, my supervisor for human rights at Harvard, contacted me about an article for one of the law school's journals. As my supervisor, Henry had commended my essay then as a work that tried to bridge Eastern and Western per-spectives. With Singapore so much in the news, Henry remembered I had won the law school's Laylin Prize for the best thesis in international law. Amidst the controversy, he had kindly suggested to the editors of the law journal that they should approach me to write for them. Having just joined the law faculty of the National University of Singapore, I was now in the business of academic writing and so I agreed.

But while Henry recommended me to the journal and told them my thesis had been awarded a prize, I was aware that events had overtaken me. The Fay caning had happened when my thesis was almost completed and I had not touched on the issues of that case. More than that, my thesis was written before the prosecution of Christopher Lingle for contempt of court. This second event, I knew, had concerned American universities because some of them felt that the Singapore action impeded the freedom of speech, sacrosanct to Americans generally and American academics particularly. I felt that the dividing lines between Singapore and the USA, East and West, between us and them, were hardening — with controversy and heated exchange. The bridge that my essay had tried to construct between the two sides might not be wide enough to traverse the increasing gap.

I cautioned the editors of the journal to read my thesis beforehand, as well as an abstract of the essay I intended to write. Were the points I would make acceptable to them? They replied that they were. The editors could not guarantee publication but as long as my essay was well-researched, as the thesis had been, the editors saw no difficulty in publishing it. With those reassurances I wrote and submitted my essay to the

Harvard journal. The editor replied to say that she liked the article and would support its publication, subject to review by another academic.

Between the time they gave me that reassurance and the final decision on publication, however, another incident brewed between America and Singapore. Williams College proposed to confer an honorary degree on Prime Minister Goh Chok Tong, and some Americans protested the decision because they saw Singapore as being anti-democratic. Leading the attack on PM Goh and Singapore was an American academic at Williams College, George Crane. When the college persisted in inviting PM Goh to receive the degree and to give a talk, Crane organised an alternative forum of critics. He invited Christopher Lingle, the American academic, fresh from evading his contempt-of-court suit in Singapore; Francis Seow, former Singapore solicitor-general and opposition candidate; and Chee Soon Juan, secretary-general of the Singapore Democratic Party. The New York columnist, William Safire, who had been so snide and often ill-informed about Singapore, declined an invitation.

With the prime minister going to the USA and publicly facing these critics, the debate between the nations seemed to reach its zenith. PM Goh held his ground. According to reports in the Singapore media, it was a minority of students at the college who protested against his award by turning their backs on the prime minister as he passed by. The protest and alternative panel went ahead, but without a big bang.

For me, too, there was no big bang. There were, however, smaller consequences. The Harvard journal replied to say that it would not publish my article. They did not say it was because of PM Goh's visit to Williams College and the ensuing controversies; moreover, manuscripts are, of course, often rejected. But less often do editors change their mind when the article is based on a thesis that they have read and an abstract that has been approved. In an apologetic e-mail, the editor explained that it was an academic reviewer who felt that my article wasn't critical enough. Not critical as being academically unsound and ill-researched? No, came the honest reply, not critical enough of Singapore.

After the prosecution of Lingle for contempt of court and after PM Goh's visit to Williams College, people had staked their sides. Singapore had its supporters in the USA, especially among the business community and those who were sick and tired of crime and felt that there was something in the Singapore approach to these issues. But those who were liberals, and involved in issues like human rights, were of a different mind-set. The Singapore government on occasion suggested that there was a conspiracy among human rights groups and the press against Singapore. Although I would not go as far as that, it was clear that the sentiment among people in this sector of America had turned against Singapore, and rejected views that were sympathetic or "not critical enough" of us. And that, to me, alone explained the journal's decision.

I was angry but powerless. I began to feel, on an individual level, what the Singapore government felt for the whole country in its debate with America, or at least certain segments in that country. I wrote to Henry

Steiner. He had, after all, supervised my thesis and suggested the article be sent. I had also known him to be a fair man, genuinely committed to human rights. It was censorship, I protested, because they did not like my viewpoint. If there were genuine points that needed amendment, this could be discussed rather than simply refusing to publish. That abuse of power in censoring me was ironic because it denied the very human rights that the journal and all liberal institutions said they sought to safeguard.

Henry responded loyally to the institution, blaming events on the hurried process of commissioning and reviewing the article. He thought the article was sound but needed some amendments. I did not write back. There was no point. It was always possible to suggest that my article simply wasn't good enough; they were Harvard and I was someone on the other side of the world, away from the centre of power and learning. In an argument between them and me, who would be believed? It was the same exercise of power that the *New York Times* had used on my reply to Safire when the Fay controversy was raging: I was free to speak, and they were free to ignore me. Despite all I had learnt about the country and its people, despite being on an American Fulbright scholarship and winning a prize for a thesis on international law at the university, there was still a price to be paid for being an alien in America, physically inside the country and yet, however, outside its consciousness. It was part of the penalty for being an Asian in this time when the East–West debate escalated across the Pacific.

I have not solved this dilemma of being an alien in America. But as for the Harvard article, I got my satisfaction. It was published by the law journal of McGill University; not as famous as Harvard's but, according to many academics, better reputed. McGill was, tellingly, a Canadian university. They were sufficiently removed from the shrill political debate between the USA and Singapore to allow an Asian voice.

❖

It was a quiet Sunday in Singapore, slightly more than a year since I returned from America. In that time, I had settled back into Singapore. I had become accustomed to the high price of cars and houses and immune to the constant complaints from my friends about such things. I had also been travelling, usually on work, to Myanmar, Cambodia, Japan, Thailand and twice to both the Philippines and Vietnam, getting to know Asia again. Over the months, I had been in contact with some of the people that I had known in the USA. Some by mail, increasing numbers by e-mail and some by phone or even in person, meeting in Singapore or elsewhere when I travelled. Such things make the globalised world of telecommunications and travel possible. You never really say goodbye to anyone that you want to keep in touch with.

Shortly after we left America, so did Karen, Linus and their kids. They did not return to Singapore, however, as we did. Linus had secured a job with a bank based in London and so they switched continents again. When Karen came back on holiday, we met at the American

Club. The move was hectic but the job and conditions for them in England were good, she said calmly, while the three children ate French fries and gulped down Coke. They were adjusting to the move; although the boys still had their American accents, Hannah – their youngest – spoke like a Sloane Ranger. They did not know how long they would be there, when they would come back. Karen, stylish and assured in her elegant black dress, seemed very comfortable with this uncertainty, the quintessential new Singaporean abroad. She invited us to visit, to stay with them again, although now in another country. We would recognise the furniture, she joked. Again, they had packed up and shipped everything over; this meant that items like their table, desk and kitchen appliances, originally from Singapore, had between more than half-way around the world.

Dave Conant, our neighbour from Vermont, came to Singapore too. It was his first visit, on the way back from studying ferns in East Malaysia. He had been in the tropical jungle for weeks as a botanist but when he stopped over in Singapore, there was just time to walk in the Botanic Gardens one afternoon before shopping and eating in a food court. It felt strange to see Dave in Singapore, walking with that rangey lope, but on Orchard Road, rather than the quiet country roads between his farm and Pingsbrooke. He got a headache from the crowds on the street.

Peter and Mei Ping too came to Singapore. Not just for a short visit like Dave, but to stay. Shortly after we left, Peter was offered a job at a new academic institution. It was a much greater challenge than things down in Philadelphia, he told us enthusiastically. Having worked in Singapore and in Asia before for quite some time, he said it felt like coming home. For Mei, she had won a prestigious art award that gave her funding just to write and to travel. She came to Singapore to be with Peter and her family. She also returned to the growing arts scene here, working with theatre groups and then teaching literature.

Ken and Danna, our friends from Cambridge, did not return to Singapore. When we had left them on a wintry day, they said that they might come out for some sun. But their plans had changed. Danna took a medical residency in New York and Ken stayed put. They travelled back and forth on weekends to be together. Although they seemed comfortable with those arrangements, I could not help but remember that warm Christmas dinner at their home, when they had just moved in and we had freshly arrived in America. I hope that they can keep the distance and loneliness of American life at bay, just as we had done that night, among friends.

Sadder news came from another couple who had helped us feel more at home in America: the Snodgrass family who had been our host family at Harvard. Shortly after we returned, Don Snodgrass wrote to tell us that Ann had died of cancer, leukemia setting in quickly despite chemotherapy. They had been kind to us during our time in America, and Ann's death just made us feel all the more privileged that we had come to know her.

I keep in touch with some classmates with the occasional postcard or letter. Some have plunged into practice on Wall Street, others are still at Harvard pursuing a doctorate, but most are back in their home countries, dispersed in the wide world they had come from. I have met two of them: Chatchom Akapin, a Thai, and Victor de Dios from the Philippines. It was different to meet them in their own countries, rather than the law school library or Harvard Square. Both were doing well in their careers; mainly because of their own hard work and good qualities, but also boosted by their Harvard qualifications. In Singapore, I received a visit from another friend from Harvard. Tony Unghie, born in Sri Lanka, now a citizen of Australia, was teaching American business law in Utah and took charge of the university's graduate studies programme. He was encouraging Asian students to go to Utah, he told me as we talked, academic to academic. Not as many as Harvard, but two Nepalese had taken his advice the year before and he had done his best to make them feel at home in Salt Lake City.

When I looked at Tony, I thought of all those like us in America, Asians passing through or staying there more permanently. I had met many of them: at Harvard, in the city, at Swarthmore and on my journeys across the country. My visit to Swarthmore College when I had met the group of young Asian Americans and gave a reading of my stories and poems, was the first time I had used the title "Alien Asian". The students had shown great interest in coming to Asia, to see first-hand the dynamic economies and growing self-assurance of the region. Some of them promised to come to Asia and Singapore in the near future, to visit or work, but very few admitted the possibility of leaving America permanently. In the enthusiasm of the time, they also said that if they did come, they wanted to look me up. And I had given a number of them my address and number.

None of them have yet come to Singapore; or, at least, none have called me. If they do, and they remind me of that meeting at Swarthmore, I would welcome them. But I am not sure I would remember their names or even recognised their faces. Here, in Asia and in Singapore, they would be strangers; the differences between us would be more obvious. There would be differences of age, of social and economic backgrounds, of accents and cultures that span the distance and variety between China, Japan and Korea, Southeast Asia and the Indian sub-continent. There would also be the fact that most of the Asians I met at Swarthmore were American citizens or permanent residents, and not aliens like me.

In Asia, in Singapore, those differences would come into focus. But in America, we were united. We were all Asians to the eye of the American mainstream. We were all alienated: I because of nationality and they because of the difference they felt from their ethnicity. It was America and what was American that created the sense of being something different, an opposite. In the months after my return to Singapore, the immediacy of my experiences have diminished, but the memory and imprint of America have not left me. Perhaps it never will because America remains – for better and for worse – a part of what makes us, in contrast, alien and Asian.

SIMON TAY is a lawyer and writer. His book of stories and poems *Stand Alone* (1991) was highly commended by the National Book Development Council of Singapore and was the first and only Singaporean book shortlisted for the Commonwealth Prize (Asia-Pacific). His two earlier books of poems, *Prism* and *5*, were also well received; *5* (1986) was highly commended by the NBDCS as a breakthrough in Singapore writing. In 1995, he received the Singaporean Young Artist Award. In 1996, he was profiled by the *Far Eastern Economic Review* in its 50th anniversary issue, citing him as one of ten persons to watch in Asia.

Born in 1961, Simon studied law at the National University of Singapore. As president of the NUS Students' Union in 1984, he led a petition against government policy. After graduation, he practised as a lawyer until 1989 when he received an International Writers' Fellowship from the University of Iowa in the USA. In 1990, he travelled through Latin America, writing a column on his experiences for the *Sunday Times*. He returned to Singapore to initiate and coordinate the Singapore Volunteers Overseas programme of the Singapore International Foundation.

In 1993, he received a Fulbright scholarship to study at Harvard University Law School. He was awarded a Master's degree in Law in 1994, winning the Laylin Prize for the best thesis in international law. While in the USA, he wrote a column for the *Straits Times*, "Fax from America". He now teaches international law at the NUS, with an emphasis on the environment and human rights.